THE DOMINICANS - A Short History

Also by Father Hinnebusch:

The Early English Friars Preachers, Rome: Istituto storico domenicano, 1951.

Dominican Spirituality. Principles and Practice. Washington, D.C.,: Thomist Press, 1965.

The History of the Dominican Order. Vol. I: Staten Island, N.Y.: Alba House, 1966. Vol. II: *ibid.,* 1973.

Renewal in the Spirit of St. Dominic. Washington, D.C.: Dominican Press, 1968.

THE DOMINICANS
A Short History

William A. Hinnebusch, O.P., D.Ph. (Oxon.)

ALBA · HOUSE NEW · YORK

SOCIETY OF ST. PAUL, 2187 VICTORY BLVD., STATEN ISLAND, NEW YORK 10314

Library of Congress Cataloging in Publication Data

Hinnebusch, William A.
   The Dominicans.
       1.   Dominicans—History
BX3506.2.H48   271'.2   74-26562
ISBN   0-8189-0301-5

Designed, printed and bound in the United States of America by the Fathers and Brothers of the Society of St. Paul, 2187 Victory Boulevard, Staten Island, New York, 10314, as part of their communications apostolate.

---

1 2 3 4 5 6 7 8 9 (*Current Printing: first digit*).

© *Copyright 1975 by the Society of St. Paul*

CONTENTS

FOREWORD 1

I. THE FOUNDATION OF THE ORDER 3

II. THE GROWTH OF THE ORDER, 1221-1303 19

III. THE MISSIONS TO 1500 47

IV. THE FOURTEENTH CENTURY 59

V. FIFTEENTH CENTURY—THE LIFE AND MINISTRY OF THE ORDER 79

VI. RENEWAL AND REFORM IN THE FIFTEENTH CENTURY 99

VII. THE SIXTEENTH CENTURY 111

VIII. THE SEVENTEENTH CENTURY, AN AGE OF ABSOLUTISM 123

IX. THE EIGHTEENTH CENTURY UNTIL 1789 137

X. THE ORDER FROM 1789 TO 1872 151

XI. THE LAST 100 YEARS, 1872 TO 1974 165

EPILOGUE 181

BIBLIOGRAPHY 183

Foreword

The stream of Dominican history is like all rivers. At times it has flowed strong and full; at times its waters have slowed to a trickle. Never has it ceased to flow. Through more than seven and a half centuries the basic ideas and fundamental inspiration of St. Dominic have vitalized the Order. In all epochs they have produced outstanding men, in some centuries an army of such men, in others only a handful. Few or many, they witnessed to the authenticity of Dominic's insights by their life and works. What the Dominican Order has given to the Church in past centuries, and what it can offer her in the future is vital and necessary, because its mission, entrusted by her—the mission to proclaim the Gospel—touches her own origins and inner being. Preaching the word of God and proclaiming the name of the Lord Jesus throughout the world will always be needed by the people of God.

It is the Order's high duty to preach, to be concerned with preaching, to wish it to be done in the best way possible, to be distressed when it is not being done, sad when it is not being done well, disappointed when another message is announced in place of God's word. The Dominican task is to study, explore, and discover better, more effective, and newer ways of disseminating the Gospel message. It will ever be the Order's duty to prepare the way for the coming or deepening of faith in those who hear the message. Everything the Dominican does, he must link to spreading the Word of God. Even when doing work that seems only distantly related to preaching, he must motivate it toward the proclamation of the word. He must therefore remain in close touch with the Scriptures, study them, pray them, guide his own life by them, and spread the good news they contain.

The reader of Dominican history who loves the Order will lament when he reads of times when the Order's river has not flown in full course. He will rejoice when its banks are filled to overflowing, when Dominican men and women in all its branches are implementing the Order's mission to the fullest of their ability.

This work is an overview rather than a detailed account of events. Its originality lies in the marshalling of the contents of Dominican history. Presenting the course of development briefly, it gives but a nod to many issues which would demand extensive treatment in a larger work. It concentrates on showing the Order's growth from the small beginnings of the thirteenth century to a world-wide presence in the twentieth.

The interest of my brethren, and the support of the provincials and councils of the three American provinces of the Order gave me the courage to undertake this work. The hospitality of my Dominican Sisters at Sparkill, New York, and at Springfield, Illinois, whose guest I was when I dictated it, the assistance of Elsie Fillio, my faithful typist, and the help of Fr. Matthew Donahue, have made an enjoyable task doubly pleasant. To all of them my thanks.

CHAPTER I

THE FOUNDATION OF THE ORDER

Dominic the Founder

St. Dominic was a spirit-filled man raised up by God to answer the pressing need of the Church for a continuous body of trained preachers. Guided by the Holy Spirit he founded the first apostolic Order, combining the contemplative consecration and apostolic ministry of the twelve apostles and the primitive Church. When Honorius III entrusted to the Order the mission to preach the Word of God, a duty that is primarily episcopal, the Church saw for the first time a religious Order with a mandate as coextensive as herself. By obtaining this universal mission, Dominic threw open the door of preaching to the members of his own Order and eventually to all Orders and priests.

Dominic took traditional elements in the Church—the apostolic life, priests living in community, regular discipline of the monastic Orders, liturgical prayer sung in community, preaching pursued in poverty—and fused them into a balanced unity that enabled his Order to meet the needs of his age and of many centuries to come.

Dominic did all his work as Founder with the full approval of the Holy See, "departing not from the teaching and the authority of the Church militant," to use the words of Pope Gregory IX. This submission to the guidance of the Church rescued his Order from suspicion and saved his sons from the errors that had nullified the good intentions of some heretical groups. Canonizing him in 1234, Gregory IX summarized Dominic's whole life when he likened him to the apostles: "I knew him as a man who followed completely the apostolic way of life. There is no doubt at all that in heaven, too, he is united with the Apostles in glory."

Though Dominic owed much to the centuries-old wisdom of monasticism, he also drew upon the experimentation and renewal that had been in progress for 150 years. From 1150 onward, a great period of reform, called the Gregorian Reform after Pope Gregory VII, had developed in the Church. It returned to the Scriptures and apostolic times as the sources of its inspiration and for the answers to great abuses, particularly among a clergy who were often ignorant, incontinent, without zeal, and who seldom preached.

Seeking to solve this problem, zealous clergy and laity endeavored to return to the simplicity and poverty of the primitive church; the apostolic life lived by the apostles became their great ideal. The clerical reformers implemented their ideas by creating the kind of religious life led by chapters of Canons Regular. They aimed to imitate the prayerful life and ministry of the apostles within a monastic framework. Chapters of Canons Regular multiplied, and several Orders developed from their ranks such as the Premonstratensians (or Norbertines), the Canons of St. Victor, and the Gilbertines. The Dominican Order, a clerical Order from the beginning, sprang from canon-regular roots.

Laymen interested in reform formed penitential brotherhoods that concentrated on poverty, penance, and preaching. In their zeal some of them fell into error, making the extreme claim that apostolic poverty is an indispensable condition for preaching and the valid administration of the sacraments. From the lay brotherhoods emerged a widespread, loose organization known as the Order of Penance, a forerunner of the later Third Order of the friars. In its earliest beginnings, the Franciscan Order shared the characteristics of these penitential brotherhoods.

The century in which Dominic was born witnessed other signs of new vigor and life besides the religious developments just described. Western Christendom enjoyed a new papal leadership, saw an expanding trade and commerce, the foundation of cities, developing vernacular languages, growing national states, and an intellectual revival. None of these movements came to maturity then, but the seeds had been planted and bore fruit during the thirteenth century, especially in Scholasticism and the infant University of Paris.

The Canons Regular filled a need in the twelfth century when they took care of the pastoral needs of the villages and rural areas where they settled. They were not equal to the task of coping with the new cities and towns of the thirteenth century. The Dominicans and Franciscans, unhampered by an existing apostolate, enjoying great flexibility, and possessing a sound theological training, settled in the cities and towns to take care of the spiritual needs of their inhabitants. In some of the thriving centers of southern France and Tuscany heresy was common. In other wealthy cities, many townsmen and the higher clergy in their love of ease and comfort posed a threat to Christian living. This love for things of the world alerted St. Dominic to the value of apostolic poverty and one of the heresies introduced him to the need Christianity faced.

Dominic was born about 1170 in the town of Caleruega in north-central Spain of Don Felix Guzman and Joan of Aza, both members of the lower nobility. From his earliest youth Dominic was trained to become a priest. Such a decision had to be made early since the choice of vocation determined the kind of training a child was given, either for knighthood or priesthood. After he had learned the rudiments, Dominic was initiated into clerical studies by his mother's brother, a priest. When he was about fourteen, he went to the cathedral school of Palencia to study philosophy and theology. He studied theology for four years, an unusually thorough formation for the average priest in those days. While in Palencia Dominic manifested his great generosity during a famine, using his slender resources to help the poor and gaining additional funds by selling his books. Completing his studies when he was about twenty-four, he joined the chapter of Canons Regular of the cathedral of Osma, and soon afterwards was ordained a priest. Later he became subprior of the chapter.

The First Steps toward Foundation

In 1203, after Dominic had spent almost ten years as a Canon

Regular, the Holy Spirit began to call him to a new vocation as founder. It seemed to happen by accident. Diego d'Acabes, his bishop, chose him as companion on an embassy to Denmark to arrange a marriage for the son of King Alfonso VIII of Castile. In passing through southern France, the travelers came to know the Albigensian heretics; in fact, the innkeeper where they stayed on their first night was a member of the sect. Dominic's zeal for souls, which had ripened during his years of contemplative life at Osma, burst into flame. He stayed up all night arguing with his host. With the rising of the sun, the man gave up his heresy and returned to the Catholic faith.

Though the bishop successfully negotiated a marriage for the King's son, the purpose of the trip was defeated when the princess died, or, as some say, entered a monastery. The bishop and Dominic discovered this two years later when they returned to her country to escort her to Spain. In Denmark the two men observed the intense missionary activity that the Danish clergy were engaged in among the pagans of the Baltic regions. Apparently aiming to join them, they went to Rome, where the bishop tendered the resignation of his diocese. Though this was not allowed and the two never again returned to the North, Dominic's missionary zeal had burst into flame and never again burned low. It became an important part of his legacy to the Order.

Pope Innocent III refused the bishop's resignation and sent him instead to work among the Albigenses. For a long time the Church had been hoping for their conversion. St. Bernard had preached to them, and Innocent had sent legates and preachers to work among them.

The bishop and Dominic obediently turned their steps westward toward France. Arriving at Montpellier, they found the papal legates, among whom was Abbot Arnauld of Citeaux, who were heartily discouraged. Despite all their efforts they had made no headway. After listening attentively, the bishop sized up the situation and gave solid advice. You must meet fire with fire. The heretic leaders live an austere life, keep long fasts, travel on foot, and preach in apostolic simplicity. "Send home your retinues then," advised the bishop, "go about on foot two by two, in imitation of the apostles, and then the Lord will bless your efforts." The bishop's zeal and arguments convinced the legates. They dismissed their retinues after Diego had set the example. They kept only "books and other necessities," as Jordan of Saxony reports. Areas for evangelization were assigned to the new groups of apostolic preachers and they set out to preach. During the following weeks and months they crisscrossed the countryside, preaching and debating with the Albigenses. After each debate, each side presented a written summary of its arguments to its opponents. The Albigenses subjected one of Dominic's summaries to a trial by fire. Three times they threw it into the fire but each time the flames cast it forth untouched.

One of the successes of Diego and Dominic was the conversion of a number of women from Albigensianism. They established a monastery for them at Prouille, near Fanjeaux, their own headquarters. This became the first monastery of the Dominican Second Order. Dominic became its father, spiritual guide, and lawgiver, a position entrusted to him by Bishop Diego when he returned to his diocese late in 1207 to recruit preachers, raise funds for the apostolate, and to regulate his diocese. He died in December soon after his return to Spain. Legate Raoul had died the previous July.

A further calamity befell the missions in January, 1208, when the Albigenses assassinated Legate Peter of Castelnau, a fiery, impatient man, who constantly antagonized them. At the end of his patience, Innocent III proclaimed a crusade against the heretics. When hostilities broke out, a peaceful apostolate became extremely difficult, but Dominic and a handful of companions persevered with their preaching despite every discouragement.

Gradually Dominic came to realize that only a religious Order could give the Church the continuous supply of trained preachers it needed. Experience had shown that volunteer preachers did not come in sufficient numbers and did not always persevere. The character of the Cathar heresy taught Dominic another lesson. Their leaders were austere, educated men, well versed in the Scriptures, who preached convincingly. These facts influenced the kind of Order Dominic founded. Its members would not only assume the usual obligations of religious but would systematically study the Scriptures.

Dominic remained true to his training and experience. Within the month that he founded the Order, he enrolled six disciples in the lecture course of Alexander Stavensby at the cathedral school of Toulouse. He himself had an excellent education and a deep love of God's word. He always carried Matthew's Gospel and Paul's Epistles. Constantly he urged the friars "by word and letter" to study the books of the Old and New Testaments. Studying the Scriptures was the medieval way of studying theology. The Bible was the chief textbook of the schools and universities. All other studies prepared the students to enter the classes of the master of theology, who unfolded the deepest meanings of the Sacred Text. Against this background, Dominic's sending seven friars to Paris in August, 1217, takes on new meaning. By preference he founded houses in university cities, at Bologna, Palencia, Montpellier, and Oxford. By design he sought to enroll university students in the Order.

The Founding of the Order

Dominic and his companions first discussed the founding of an Order seriously during 1213 and 1214 at Fanjeaux. In the spring of 1215 they were ready, and Bishop Fulk of Toulouse established them as a preaching brotherhood for his diocese. Dominic gave vows to Thomas and Peter Seila, citizens of Toulouse. Seila deeded some houses he owned to the Order. The larger became the Order's first priory when Dominic and the brethren took up their residence there. Soon afterwards the bishop gave the church of St. Romanus for their community prayers. Thus the Order of Preachers began on a small scale with episcopal approval.

The next step was to obtain papal confirmation of the foundation. The opportunity came when Bishop Fulk set out for Rome in 1215, with Dominic in his company, to attend the Fourth Lateran Council.

Jordan describes their project: "They petitioned the Lord Pope Innocent to confirm for Brother Dominic and his disciples an

Order that would be an Order of Preachers; likewise that he would confirm the revenues that had been assigned to the brothers by the count and by the bishop." A hurdle to confirmation had to be faced. On the agenda for the Council was a proposal to prohibit the founding of new religious Orders. To surmount it, Innocent advised Dominic to choose one of the existing religious Rules. He promised that when this had been done, he would confirm the Order.

In the spring of 1216, Dominic and the friars chose the Rule of St. Augustine and framed statutes to supplement it. These became the first half of the permanent Constitutions of the Order. Adapted from the Constitutions of Premontre, they regulated the religious life of the friars. Nothing was legislated until four years later to govern the Order's apostolate. Dominic wisely waited to learn from experience what laws and organization would best suit a preaching Order. In October, the friars added to the property of St. Romanus' church and began to build "a cloister with cells above it suitable for study and sleeping." Returning to Rome, Dominic "obtained to the fullest extent both the confirmation of his Order as he conceived it as well as the other things he desired." On December 22, Honorius III (Innocent had died in July) granted a bull of confirmation, approving the Order as a body of Canons Regular. A second bull, issued on January 21, 1217, recognized the newness of Dominic's ideas and approved his foundation as "an Order that would be called and would be an Order of Preachers." Honorius addressed its members as "Christ's unconquered athletes, armed with the shield of faith and the helmet of salvation. Fearing not those who can kill the body, you valiantly thrust the word of God which is keener than any two-edged sword, against the foes of the faith."

The Order's Charism

The Order of Preachers was an entirely new kind of religious Order. For the first time an Order incorporated as an integral part of its religious life a ministry that shared the bishop's fundamental duty to preach the word of God, a mission conferred by the Holy Father, the universal bishop of the Church. The Order seeks to place at the service of the bishops a body of educated and trained preachers prepared to assist them in the laborious duty of preaching. The Lateran Council called on bishops to appoint just such cooperators with themselves to remedy the long-standing need of the Church for regular and competent preaching, especially in the towns and cities. Eventually the preaching ministry was opened to other Orders, but it has remained the vocation of the Order of Preachers to be concerned that the preaching needs of the Church be met. Preaching remains its special mission and duty.

Shortly before or after the bull of January 21, which granted this mission, Dominic had a vision of the apostles Peter and Paul while he was praying in the old church of St. Peter that was prophetic. Peter handed him a preacher's staff and Paul the book of Gospels, saying to him, "Go and preach; for this you have been sent." Then he saw his sons going two by two through the world preaching.

The vision of Dominic was authentic and captured the genius, spirit, and purpose of the Dominican Order. It repeated in a dramatic way the ideas Pope Honorius expressed in one of the very earliest bulls he issued to the Order:

God Who continually makes His Church fruitful in new children, wishing to bring our times into conformity with earlier days and spread the Catholic faith has inspired you to embrace a life of poverty and regular discipline and to devote yourselves to preaching the word of God and proclaiming the name of our Lord Jesus Christ throughout the world.

The bull of January 21, the vision of Peter and Paul, and perhaps the discouraging conditions in southern France determined Dominic to scatter his friars to the four winds. Both they and his friends tried to dissuade him. "It seemed to their worldly prudence," Jordan of Saxony wrote, "that he was tearing down rather than raising up the building that he had started." Dominic's answer was: "Seed when scattered fructifies, when hoarded, rots." He urged his men to go without fear, promising that he would pray for them and they would succeed. On August 15,

1217, the day of Our Lady's Assumption, he sent seven to Paris "to study, preach, and found a priory," and four to Spain. Three stayed in Toulouse and two at Prouille to help the sisters. He himself remained in the area until December 13, when he left for Rome. As he passed through Milan and Bologna, he prepared for future foundations.

Growth and Organization

From December until mid-May Dominic was in Rome, consulting about his Order, preaching and obtaining a series of letters of recommendation for presentation to the bishop when the friars arrived in a city to make a foundation. The letters show Dominic's reliance on the Holy Father, help us trace the opening of houses in France, Germany, Spain, and Italy, and reaffirm the Order's name, mission, and voluntary poverty.

In Rome, Dominic took Reginald of Orleans into the Order. A magnetic man, powerful preacher, teacher and administrator, Reginald had a distinguished career as professor and diocesan official behind him when he became a friar. Soon afterwards he became seriously ill with a burning fever, but Dominic's prayer gained his recovery. The Blessed Mother appeared, anointed Reginald, and approved his new vocation by showing him the Dominican habit. Later that year his leadership and preaching made the community at Bologna, founded at this time by Dominic, the equal of Paris in strength and influence.

When Dominic left Rome in May, 1218, he began a visitation that occupied him until July, 1219, and carried him through Italy, southern France, Spain and Paris to Bologna. As he went, he admitted new members and founded new houses: Bologna, Lyons, Segovia, Montpellier, Bayonne, Limoges, and perhaps Reims and Metz. In Paris he discovered thirty friars who were taking full advantage of the educational and preaching opportunities presented by the university city. Besides, Jordan of Saxony, a bachelor of theology who was destined to be his successor, declared his intention of joining the Order. It had been a most fruitful year. Not only had the number of men and houses increased, but Dominic had amassed a wealth of data and experience about the Order: how the friars lived the religious life and implemented their mission, how they observed poverty, and what kind of laws were needed to establish good government and guide the ministry.

In Bologna Dominic was delighted to find that the fledgling community he had founded a year before had, under Reginald's guidance, become a strong, vigorous group of students and scholars of reputation, such as Roland of Cremona. Dominic now took personal charge at Bologna, sending Reginald as superior to Paris. Within a few months of his arrival, before he could repeat his experience at Bologna, Reginald died. However, Providence provided a successor for him and Dominic, when Jordan of Saxony took vows in his hands. Jordan outstripped both of them in the thousand or more men he recruited during the years he was master general, from 1222 to 1237.

Dominic was now ready for the final, most fruitful years of his life. He took steps that gave his Order stability and a sense of identity, rooted in a definite mission and a clear understanding of the means to achieve it. Contributing not a little to this effect was the formation of an excellent set of laws and an efficient government. Preliminary to these results were several visits to the papal court at Viterbo, a new series of papal letters of recommendation, and a stay of several months in Rome, during which he supervised the organization of the monastery of San Sisto (a work entrusted to him by the pope). These works occupied him from late October, 1219, until May, 1220. Meanwhile, he sent out letters calling representatives of the priories to meet in general chapter at Bologna in May.

The time was ripe for this step; whereas in 1216, when there were only one or two houses and a handful of men, none had the experience and knowledge to devise laws for an Order that for the first time in history combined the contemplative life with a general active ministry, now Dominic's ideas had been tested by experience and his tour of visitation had prepared him to devise a government for a world-wide Order incorporating laws for preaching, formation of new members, studies, and poverty. By summoning a chapter of brethren, he declared his intention to proceed democratically through representation and consultation.

The 1220 General Chapter

With the opening of the first general chapter on Pentecost Sunday, May 17, 1220, the two major elements of Dominican government were in existence—the office of Master General and the Chapter.

When the Chapter began Dominic startled the delegates by tendering his resignation: "I deserve to be removed from office, as I am unfit for the post and remiss," a mixture of humility and fact. After the Chapter was over, his personal guidance would no longer be indispensable. The Order would be able to stand alone. Furthermore, his health was failing. Years of exhausting labor, severe asceticism, and constant traveling had left their mark. The friars refused to hear of his resignation; therefore he deferred to their will but stipulated that while in session the chapter would be supreme. He also would be subject to it. This is still the case. Though presiding, the master general is but first among equals. Each shares authority and has a vote of equal weight. The chapter is the supreme executive, legislative, and judiciary authority in the Order.

The 1220 chapter added a prologue to the Constitutions, granting superiors the important power of dispensation:

> *The prelate shall have power to dispense the brethren in his priory when it shall seem expedient to him, especially in those things that are seen to impede study, preaching, or the good of souls, since it is known that our Order was especially founded from the beginning for preaching and the salvation of souls. Our study ought to tend principally, ardently, and with the highest endeavor to the end that we might be useful to the souls of our neighbors.*

This text crystallizes the Dominican mission and spirit. It aims to facilitate the Order's ministry and reconcile its demands with those of the religious life. Both are necessary to achieve the

Order's purpose, yet exist in a natural state of tension—it takes effort to harmonize the life of a contemplative and the activity of an evangelist—a tension that exists in the Church herself, who is "eager to act and yet devoted to contemplation" (Vatican II, SL 2).

Dominic did not set up an impossible standard when he coupled the consecrated life of prayer and the ministry. He himself harmonized both and a realistic view of his life does much to relieve the tension. Though he was Spirit-led and enjoyed great gifts of prayer, the record shows that the basic qualities of his contemplation can be matched by any Dominican. Gerald Vann could have had him in mind when he wrote: "To be a contemplative man is to be a prayerful person; that means to be thoughtful before God." Dominic prayed at night and during the day. He preached, worked, and traveled, but took the time to pray. Always he was "thoughtful before God."

Even so, tension remains when a man faces two sets of demands that cannot be met at the same moment. To take care of this practical situation, Dominic created the functional dispensation (an innovation in the religious life), given to facilitate study, the ministry, and the salvation of men. Besides, dispensation gives his sons the assurance that when they study, preach, or do any work of the ministry, they are serving God and keeping the Constitutions as well as when they stand in chapel. Dispensation gives them flexibility, mobility, and the liberty of the sons of God, free to do his work. To increase this freedom, Dominic made it clear that the Order's laws of themselves do not bind under sin.

Dominic wanted Gospel men in his Order. The Church gave it the mission to proclaim God's word, and Dominic knew from experience that this word can be proclaimed rightly only when it has been prayerfully pondered before God. Though he prescribed systematic study of the Scriptures, he understood that God's word is a heavenly reality that cannot be fathomed by a purely intellectual process; its proclamation must be the fruit of prayerful savoring that becomes love when it matures. He wanted his sons to be prayerful men who had experienced the word. Coupled with study, their prayerful life was the condition of their becoming apostles.

The 1220 chapter completed its work by passing laws for preaching, study, poverty, visitation and organization of the priories, and the procedure of general chapters. By requiring that each priory have a professor it laid the foundation for the Order's schools. It also tightened the Order's poverty. In 1216 the men had decided "not to own possessions lest concerns for temporal things impede the preaching ministry ... for the time being [the Order would] retain only revenues." The chapter ruled that "possessions and revenues are not to be accepted under any circumstances." The Order would trust in God's providence and the offerings of the faithful. Preachers would go out in pairs as Gospel men, traveling on foot, and "neither accepting nor carrying gold, silver, money, or gifts, except for food, and books."

The chapter had completed its work. Under Dominic's skillful hand, the representatives, probably not more than thirty, among them theologians from Paris and canon and civil lawyers from Bologna, had done a superb work. They had given the Order a strong government and wise laws to guide its ministry. Dominic's work would endure.

After the chapter ended, Dominic plunged into a preaching campaign as head of a papal mission sent to preach in northern Italy. His own tours in Lombardy enabled him to visit the priories at Milan and Bergamo, and perhaps prepare for one in Piacenza. Upon returning to Bologna, he decided to found a monastery for Diana d'Andalo and her companions. Under his guidance, she had vowed in 1219 to enter the religious life. Though he entrusted the project to four friars before he left for Rome in December, the monastery could not be founded until after his death.

Dominic stayed in Rome until mid-May, 1221. He went to report to the Pope on his preaching in Lombardy, to deal with the Papal curia about the Order's affairs, and establish the nuns at San Sisto. He preached in the churches, talked with recluses, and instructed the nuns at San Sisto and the friars at Santa

Sabina, the friars who had gone there in February, 1221. Dominic also sent two friars to Siena in March, planned foundations in Metz, Spires, and Lund, and received papal letters of recommendation to the bishops of Amiens and Piacenza and the people of Sigtuna, Sweden, and obtained for the Order the privilege of using a portable altar. Now the friars could set up a temporary chapel while awaiting the completion of their church and need not hold their services in the parish church.

The Chapter of 1221

The second general chapter convened under Dominic's presidency at Bologna on May 30, 1221. Though we do not have a detailed account of its work, we do know that it created the province and its chapter as an intermediate form of government and ministry. The Order's government now embodied its principles of collegiality and subsidiarity, so highly valued in our country. Also, during the sessions Dominic made another innovation in monastic practice, declaring that the Order's laws do not bind under sin. Some years later, when friars who had not known him began to doubt this, the 1235 chapter put it in writing. Dominic respected the freedom of his sons as children of God, expecting them to act responsibly under the prompting of the Holy Spirit and not through fear of sin. The trust that runs like a golden thread through the government and life of the Order is featured by collegiality, subsidiarity, and accountability, Dominic's gifts to his sons. In these matters the Dominican heart beats in time with the pulse of the thirteenth century, a period noted for the introduction of representative procedures into state and municipal governments and the proliferation of voluntary and local associations—guilds, charitable organizations, confraternities, and universities. All of them employed elective and representative methods of government.

The province, governed by a provincial and a provincial chapter, is a subdivision of the Order and unites groups of priories in one administrative unit. Each priory in the province was given the right to send its prior and an elected delegate to represent it at the provincial chapter. The assembly cannot enact constitutions but, acting on information brought by priors and delegates, it may issue ordinances and admonitions regarding the religious life, study, teaching, and the work of the ministry. It elects the provincial and supervises the conduct of the friars, of its provincial, priors, professors, and students, and may send petitions to the general chapter. One of the chapter's permanent elements was the presence of preachers general. They were outstanding preachers (one was appointed for each priory) and brought their wisdom and experience to the chapter's deliberations. After 1407 masters of theology joined them. Especially the presence of the masters, whose numbers were theoretically unlimited, weakened the democratic character of the chapter. The constantly changing membership of the chapter harnesses the wisdom, experience, and ideas of a wide spectrum of friars in providing for the good of the province, Order, and Church.

Until modern times, as provinces grew in size they were subdivided into visitations. The provincial appointed a visitator to inspect these subdivisions, judge their performance and make recommendations to the provincial chapter. Each visitation also included certain schools as we shall see later.

The priory was the most important and smallest administrative and territorial division of the Order in medieval times. Though under the jurisdiction of the province, it was self-governing and held various rights, privileges, and obligations. Governed by a prior, who was elected by the community, it established the atmosphere in which the friar lived and from which he carried out his ministry. When the spirit of priories was high, the province and Order functioned well; when the morale was low, the province and Order were paralyzed and functioned with difficulty.

The general chapters after 1221 completed the Constitutions, so that by 1228, the Order boasted a completely developed system of government. It was well integrated and well balanced between monarchical elements of the administration and democratic elements of community control. Collegiality, subsidiarity, and representation were among its prominent features. When functioning properly, the Dominican Constitutions promote the Order's work, pay due regard to the ideas and desires of the friars, and impart a flexibility that enables the Order to expand its membership, territory, and kinds of work. It adjusts itself to new times and new societies by its own legislative action.

The Death of Dominic

Dominic filled the last six weeks of his life, following the second general chapter, with intense preaching throughout Lombardy. When he returned to Bologna at the end of July, he was burning with fever. He died on the feast of the Transfiguration, August 6, 1221. He had planned so wisely, governed so prudently, and structured the Order's government so well, that the Order could survive without him. He was laid to rest under the feet of his brethren in the chapel at Bologna. Gregory IX canonized him on July 3, 1234, comparing him as he did so to the apostles and to the great founders, Benedict, Bernard, Francis. His flame has never gone out.

CHAPTER II

THE GROWTH OF THE ORDER, 1221-1303

The thirteenth was the greatest Dominican century. Full of life and enthusiasm, the Order attracted or developed men of outstanding ability. Its ideals and methods were in harmony with the times and were characterized by an inner strength that had not yet lost its initial verve and momentum. This strength, reinforced by an explosive expansion of membership, enabled the Order to enter new areas of ministry. While Dominic still lived it made foundations in France, Italy, Spain, Germany, and Scandinavia. Under his presidency the second general chapter, 1221, divided Europe into eight provinces and sent friars to Hungary, Poland, and England. When Dominic died there were about twenty priories and perhaps 300 friars.

Growth during the next thirty-five years was phenomenal. From a letter Humbert of Romans sent to King Louis IX of France in 1256, we can deduce that there were 10,000 priests. Probably we could add 3,000 novices, students, and cooperator brothers. The total enrollment would then stand at 13,000. Fragmentary statistics indicate that the membership was about 12,600 when the century ended. The general chapter ordered a census in 1336 but, if taken, no figures have survived. After the Black Death had done its work (1348-1349), membership of the Order and clergy was sharply reduced. Unsettled conditions generally made recruiting difficult during the remaining years of the medieval period.

We can also measure the Order's growth by consulting three catalogues of priories. The first, from 1277, lists twelve provinces and 404 priories. The second, from 1303, shows eighteen provinces and 590 priories. On the 1358 list there are no new provinces, but priories have increased to 630. Growth slowed down then until colonization began in America and Asia. After 1358, the three provinces of France established fewer than twenty new priories; the two German provinces exhibit the same growth rate. Only one priory was founded in England. The province of Scandinavia remained stationary.

Monasteries of Dominican nuns jumped from the four in existence when Dominic died (Prouille, San Sisto, Madrid, and St. Stephen of Gormaz in Spain) to fifty-eight in 1277, 141 in 1303, and 157 in 1358. Nuns of other monasteries followed the Order's laws and wore its habit, but were under the bishop's jurisdiction. Often the Order provided for them spiritually.

As the number of friars and priories increased, the provinces began to find administration cumbersome, but until the end of the century the inherent unwillingness of organizations to fragment their own strength nullified the attempts of the general chapters to divide them. In 1294 the King of Sicily had the Pope separate the Dominicans of his kingdom from the province of Rome and established them as a province. Between 1301 and 1303, the province of Aragon was carved from the province of Spain, Bohemia from Poland, Saxony from Germany, and Toulouse from Provence. It was late in the fourteenth century before any new provinces were added to the roll.

Dominican Leadership and Life

The strong sense of self-identity the Order inherited from Dominic aided its growth and development. The qualities of this identity were a spirit of prayer, a thirst for the salvation of men, love for the Scriptures, an appreciation of study and learning, and a sharp awareness of its preaching mission and the ways to achieve it. A family spirit and unbroken unity were the results. During the century two new elements heightened this sense of identity and unity: a unified liturgy and the theology of Thomas.

The Order was fortunate in the first five successors of Dominic —Jordan of Saxony (1222-1237), Raymond of Penyafort (1238-1240), John of Wildeshausen (1241-1252), Humbert of Romans

(1254-1263), and John of Vercelli (1264-1283). Men of ability, learning and remarkable goodness (the Church has canonized Raymond and beatified Jordan and Vercelli), they respected the original inspiration of the Founder, yet they encouraged sound growth and built wisely on the foundations he had laid. During their terms of office, the Order's basic development took place, especially during the tenure of Jordan. Under them, the Order organized and expanded its academic system and its ministries: preaching, foreign missions, and service to the Church and people. After the last of them had died, there were twenty-five years during which the generals ruled for so short a period or encountered such difficulties that they were unable to provide the forceful leadership of their predecessors. They were Munio of Zamora (1258-1291), Stephen of Besançon (1292-1294), Nicholas Boccasino (1296-1298), who has been beatified, Albert Chiavari (1300), and Bernard of Jusix (1301-1303). During this period, the Order's original vitality weakened and its momentum became sluggish.

The many friars who became bishops soon after Dominic's death evoked fear that talented men would continually be lost to the Order. Jordan of Saxony tried to reverse the trend by forbidding friars to accept election to the bishopric without permission. However, he could not control the popes; friars continued to enter the hierarchy. In 1244 Innocent IV created Hugh of St. Cher cardinal, the first Dominican to receive the red hat. Before the medieval period ended, Peter of Tarentaise (Bl. Innocent V) and Nicholas Boccasino (Bl. Benedict XI) reigned as popes, twenty-eight Dominicans became cardinals, and many served as bishop. Others occupied the office of master of the sacred palace (the theologian of the papal curia), functioned as penitentiaries or chaplains, and worked in lesser posts at the papal court. Raymond of Penyafort, papal penitentiary and able canonist, made a memorable contribution to the Church when he codified its laws. Commissioned by Gregory IX in 1230 and promulgated by him in 1234 as the sole official code of the Church, the collection bears the title *Decretals of Gregory IX*.

Dominican theologians and bishops took part in the general councils of the medieval centuries. Tangible evidence of the

Order's contribution to the second Council of Lyons (the first at which there was a notable Dominican presence) is the treatise Humbert of Romans prepared in response to Gregory X's invitation to bishops and generals. He devoted attention to the objectives the Holy Father set for the Council—security of the Holy Land, union of the Orthodox and Catholic Churches, and reform. Thirty Dominican bishops attended, among them Albert the Great, and some of the Order's theologians. William of Moerbeke, who had worked in Greece as a missionary, and John of Constantinople, a Franciscan, led the chanting of the Creed in both Latin and Greek to celebrate the union of the Churches that was achieved by the Council. William, a noted translator of early Greek works, rendered some of them into Latin "at the request of Friar Thomas Aquinas." Thomas died while journeying to the Council.

Besides St. Dominic, the Church has canonized the following medieval Dominicans: Hyacinth, Peter of Verona, Margaret of Hungary, Raymond of Penyafort, Albert the Great, Thomas Aquinas, Agnes of Montepulciano, Catherine of Siena, Vincent Ferrer, and Antoninus. In addition, the Order venerates twenty-one friars, seventeen Dominican women, Joan of Aza, the mother of Dominic, two groups of martyrs, and five individual martyrs.

In 1233 Jordan of Saxony removed the relics of Dominic from the brick vault where they had rested since 1221 and placed them in a plain marble tomb. In 1267 John of Vercelli transferred them to a sarcophagus ornamented with bas-reliefs, attributed to Niccolo Pisano (probably aided by William of Pisa, a cooperator brother), depicting the role of Dominic as apostle and founder. Though the tomb reflects the position of influence and popularity the Order had reached in its fifth decade, it also symbolizes its departure from the simplicity that Dominic had wanted, and it had practiced in its earlier days. The tomb gradually assumed its present form as the result of many transformations and additions, contributed by noted sculptors, among them Michelangelo. The contemporary tomb of Peter of Verona, still standing in Milan, represents the original form of Dominic's 1267 tomb.

The Order's Government and Laws

The general chapters between Dominic's death and 1228 perfected the machinery of government for the Order and provinces, granted provinces more autonomy and chapters more control over elected officials, balanced and safeguarded the relative powers of provincials and diffinitors in general chapters, and provided a method of making laws through the action of three successive chapters. In addition, they prohibited riding on horseback, carrying money when traveling, and eating meat. The chapter of 1228 made many of these additions and added four new provinces. It and the 1236 chapter were most general, i.e., equivalent in authority and composition to three ordinary chapters. From 1245 cities such as Cologne, Montpellier, Trier, London, Budapest, and Metz played host to these assemblies that brought friars from all over Europe. When he was master general, Raymond of Penyafort made it easier to consult the Constitutions by putting them in a more logical and juridical form. His arrangement endured until 1924, when the Order brought its laws into harmony with the 1918 Code of Canon Law.

If Raymond codified the laws of the Order, Humbert of Romans crystallized its spirit. The books he wrote after he resigned as master general have had a marked influence on the Dominican character. They enshrine his thought and rich experience. He dealt with the religious life, compiled materials and sermon outlines for preachers, and suggested solutions for contemporary ecclesiastical problems. His influence on later generations came from his long ascetical exposition of the Rule of St. Augustine, an unfinished commentary on the Constitutions, and a book on the offices of the Order. In this last book he ranged from the master general down to the porter of a priory, detailing the duties of all offices and how they should be performed. Printed editions of the Constitutions carried this work until the last century. The semi-official acceptance of it and the commentaries indicates that the Order looked on them as outstanding descriptions of its spirit and ministry.

The Dominican Rite

The Order's drive to attain a single liturgy for itself underscores its esteem for the worship of God and its own prayer life. The drive for a unified liturgy, apparently begun during the days of Dominic, resulted very early in the fashioning of a primitive Dominican Rite and breviary. Demands for greater uniformity led to the appointment of a four-friar commission in 1245, whose revisions, though accepted in 1248, proved to be unsatisfactory. Therefore the 1254 chapter entrusted Humbert of Romans, just elected general, with a further revision. He finished it in 1256 and that year's chapter confirmed it. Clement IV gave ecclesiastical approval in 1267. Enduring until the liturgical revisions that followed Vatican II, the Dominican Rite forged a link in family unity.

The Friars and the Nuns

The Order solved another family problem during this time. After Dominic died, the Order's monasteries increased so rapidly that many friars feared the preaching ministry would be harmed. How serious the threat was can be seen from the custom of stationing some friars at the monasteries to care for the spiritual and temporal welfare of the nuns. As this ministry claimed increasing numbers of men, at the petition of Master General Raymond of Penyafort, the Holy See exempted the Order from this charge. When San Sisto in Rome and St. Agnes in Bologna, two of the oldest monasteries, appealed this decision, the Pope declared the ruling inapplicable to them. Then, when all seemed settled, Cardinal Hugh of St. Cher, papal legate in Germany, opened the flood gates again. He ordered the German Dominicans to care for the monasteries as before. John of Wildeshausen laid the problem before the 1252 general chapter. It enumerated the priorities: work for souls, foreign missions, the claims of study, and crusade preaching. Supervision of the nuns was not a top priority. Innocent IV took the side of the chapter. Only Prouille and San Sisto might have friars to assist them. Other monasteries could keep the habit and Rule but not demand Dominican help.

It was a hollow victory. The nuns won their point in 1267 when Clement IV placed the monasteries under the general's jurisdiction. It was a compromise. The Order would take care of the nuns spiritually, preaching and hearing confessions, but would have no responsibility for their temporal welfare. The bond of unity thus restored was not broken even when the Council of Trent placed all nuns under the jurisdiction of the bishops.

Even before the dispute with the nuns was settled, Humbert of Romans moved toward unifying their life. Until then they had lived under the primitive Constitutions imparted to Prouille by St. Dominic. This code was known as the Rule of San Sisto. The sisters added statutes to it between 1228 and 1232 to bring their life into greater conformity with that of the fathers and brothers. In addition, masters general and provincials issued local statutes to individual monasteries. To bring order to this disarray of documents, Humbert promulgated revised Constitutions for the nuns in 1259. Imposed on all the monasteries, it remained their law until 1932.

The Pastoral Crisis

While these family problems were moving toward solution, the Order entered its first crisis. The friars had expected that they would cooperate with bishops and pastors. This was the intention of the Church. Many bishops and parish priests welcomed them, but after 1240 the hostility of many of the clergy toward the new Order became evident. The growing number of friars, their organization of the preaching ministry, and their success caused opposition. As bishops and priests realized that the friars exercised a ministry that was beyond their control, many of them severely hampered the work of the mendicant Orders (a name referring to the strict poverty of the friars). By mid-century the dispute reached crisis proportions. The attack threatened the very life of the Dominicans and Franciscans.

The controversy revolved mainly around the exemption of the friars from episcopal control, their privileges, and their ministry, especially preaching and its financial rewards. If the attack had succeeded, the originality of the new Orders would have been destroyed and the development of the religious life set back for centuries. However, the popes came to the support of the friars. The Church had created the Orders and found them a valuable arm in furthering its policies.

The danger became acute when the University of Paris joined the conflict, seeking to terminate the teaching of the friars. In November 1254, Innocent IV, prompted by William of St. Amour and delegates of the University, revoked the friars' privileges and subjected their ministry to the local clergy. However, their victory was short-lived. Two weeks later Innocent was dead and the friars claimed they had prayed him into his grave. Alexander IV canceled the bull of Innocent one month after it had been issued.

The controversy over hearing confessions went back and forth until 1281, when Martin IV granted Dominicans and Franciscans who were licensed by their superiors power to hear confessions everywhere without seeking further authorization. He not only sustained the ministry of the friars but officially approved the liberty of the faithful to confess to any priest who had jurisdiction, provided they confessed once a year to their own priest. It was a step toward greater freedom of conscience and more fruitful use of the Sacrament of Penance. Still the controversy continued. In 1300 a statesman-like compromise of Boniface VIII solved some of the pressing problems of the conflict, conceding something to each side. The friars might preach without hindrance, except when a bishop was preaching, or a sermon was delivered in his presence. For hearing confessions, the prior was to present to the bishop priests capable of administering this sacrament. Should he refuse to accept these candidates, they might proceed to preach and hear confessions. In either case authorization came from the pope. This procedure was required for a valid use of the authority granted. Though the decision of Boniface was a workable compromise, the controversy simmered until the Council of Trent established the present law, under which priests must apply to the bishop for authority.

The dispute with the diocesan clergy was necessary. Had they not threatened to submerge the friars in the parochial system, the friar Orders would not have become as strong and useful as they did. Though the ministry of the friars was under attack, the pope safeguarded it by granting them a complexus of rights and privileges that exempted them from episcopal control and guaranteed them an efficiency, mobility, and flexibility they did not have when they were founded. The preaching and sacramental work of the friars, the counsel and help they gave the faithful were removed beyond the interference of the diocesan clergy. As ultimately developed, mendicant privileges extended to the following points: direct dependence on the Holy See, exemption of the internal affairs of the Order from episcopal control, the right to erect churches and public oratories, the privilege of burying the faithful in their cemeteries, freedom from paying tithes on legacies, funeral fees, and bequests, the right to teach theology in their own priories and at the Universities.

The controversy served another purpose. The secular clergy acted as a counterweight to the mendicant movement. Without such a balance the friars might have completely disrupted the ecclesiastical organization. They had to be assimilated but not the way the clergy intended. The strength of the friars, nourished by papal support, was dynamic enough to withstand the attack. By forcing them to turn to the popes, the opposition prevented the friars from drifting towards extreme doctrinal positions that had carried other movements, such as that of the Humiliati, Waldenses, and Fraticelli, into heresy.

In summarizing, we should note the following factors. The Order relied on prayer during this crisis, commanding litanies and prayers to be recited during the height of the controversy with the University of Paris. It sought to establish closer collaboration with the Franciscans, and advised the friars to use their privileges moderately and make agreements with the local clergy. Finally, it worked in close dependence on the Holy See.

Intellectual Training and Doctrinal Mission

Dominic laid the foundation for the Order's doctrinal mission and is the founder of its system of schools. He sought to ensure a solid theological training for his sons. The Constitutions drawn up under his presidency in 1220 called for the founding of a theological school in each priory and regulated the activity of professors and students.

As the Order grew numerically and geographically, it built an elaborate scholastic organization that provided a network of schools; priory schools, provincial schools of philosophy and theology, and a graduate program pursued at general houses of studies, usually associated with universities.

The schools developed first at the lowest and highest levels —priory schools and general houses of studies. Classes began as soon as a priory was established. When Dominic died there were about fifteen priories; in 1227, when the first census was taken there were 404. Evidence shows that the Constitutions were observed, and a professor was appointed in each priory. Thus in 1277 there were 404 Dominican schools of theology in existence.

The general house of studies was a school where select students studied advanced theology. The roots of the Paris general house were grounded in 1227 when the friars arrived and John of St. Albans, a secular master, was engaged to teach. When Roland of Cremona graduated in 1229, the Order obtained its first chair of theology. It acquired a second the following year when John of St. Giles, a secular master, became a Dominican. About the same time another secular master, Robert Bacon, took the habit in England, giving the Oxford *studium* its chair.

A quota system permitted each province to send three students to Paris. When it could no longer accomodate all the students who wanted to come, as the Order grew in numbers, a partial solution was found in the creation of provincial houses of theology. A more far-reaching solution was a mandate of the 1248 general chapter commanding four additional general houses to be founded: at Oxford, Bologna, Montpellier, and Cologne. Each province might send two students to each.

Although this mandate was probably not immediately implemented in all four places, the legislation itself was extremely important. Albert Hauck, a German historian, brought out its full significance, pointing out, first, that the founding of the four *studia* was important in its primary intent, namely, a great religious corporation had solved its academic problems. Until then no one else had attempted such a thorough solution; instead chance had usually had full play in academic matters. Secondly, by gathering advanced students preparing for the professorship into selected houses of studies, the Order distinguished between advanced theological work and theological preparation for the ministry; scholarship was given an independent right. Thirdly, since the new houses of studies were restricted to the theological disciplines, the Order took a giant step toward categorizing the sciences. Theology took its place as a special field of learning for the first time.

Additional general houses of studies were founded late in the thirteenth century. The 1304 general chapter ordered all the provinces, with the exception of three small ones, to found a general house of studies. When this order was implemented there were fifteen Dominican general houses of studies in Europe. The close bond between these schools and the universities kept Dominicans in the path of the intellectual current sweeping through Europe. In fact, until the middle of the fifteenth century, the Holy See restricted the teaching of theology, outside of Paris and Oxford, to the houses of studies of the mendicant friars.

In 1259 the Order promulgated its first academic code at the general chapter meeting at Valenciennes, completing its academic organization. The code was the work of five masters of theology, Albert the Great, Thomas Aquinas, Peter of Tarentaise, Florence of Hesdin, and Bonhomme of Brittany. These masters were appointed by the chapter to draw up the code, which was occasioned by academic developments at the University of Paris, whose Faculty of Arts had broadened its philosophical courses in 1255. In a brief and concise document, the commission of five masters regulated many aspects of Dominican studies. In the 1240's and 1250's two provinces had permitted some of their schools to introduce philosophy courses, a step made necessary by the increasing interest in the subject caused by the introduction of works of Aristotle and other eastern writers. The code legislated for a development that was already in progress, authorizing the general establishment of schools of philosophy. This was a progressive step, acknowledging dialectics and logic as legitimate tools of theological speculation, a step taken in full accord with the most advanced trends in the field of thought. It completed the Dominican academic network. The road down which Dominic had walked when he led his first disciples to the courses of Alexander of Stavensby had been followed to its logical destination.

The 1259 code provided for academic exercises in the schools similar to those of the universities: lectures, disputations, determinations, and repetitions. It set down the duties of lectors, bachelors, priors, student masters, visitators, and students. The five masters designated a method of choosing students for advanced courses, safeguarded the rights and privileges of lectors and students, took measures to prevent them from being distracted from their studies, permitted them to be dispensed from certain other duties, required them, and even priors and lectors who were not currently teaching, to frequent classes regularly. They stipulated what books students were to take to lectures and made provisions for their support. The ordinances also provided machinery for the regular supervision of studies. The Constitutions had commanded the visitators, sent out annually to the priories, to inquire into academic matters. The code amplified these duties, directing them to recommend friars for advanced studies and to determine whether lectors were faithful to their classes, held disputations, and gave magistral solutions to problems. They were obliged to report to the provincial chapter and notify it when a priory needed a professor. Because of the training imparted under the code, Dominican students coming to the general houses of studies for advanced work encountered no difficulty in being accepted at the universities as fully qualified, able to stand on an equal footing with students who had completed their courses in the Faculty of Arts.

The study of philosophy had raised the same questions and

problems in the Order as it did in the Church. Older, more conservative friars, questioned whether it should be studied at all. Other scholars, like John of St. Giles, who were aware of the necessity of philosophy for the scientific study of theology, vacillated in their approach to the eastern philosophers. While not opposed to philosophy, they cautioned theologians against the excessive cult of Aristotle. Others, like Vincent of Beauvais, peppered their writings with numerous quotations from Aristotle but did so with apologies and qualms of conscience. The code marked the victory of Albert the Great and the masters, who, with the full support of Master General Humbert of Romans, had advocated the use of philosophy in theological studies. The career of Thomas, his literary productivity, and the excellence of his works, paralleling the enforcement of the code, are a concrete witness to the value of philosophy. The code's implementation promised the Order a succession of scholars and theologians and assured them a place in the vanguard of theological thought. It manifests how completely the Order had accepted its doctrinal mission.

The Teaching Ministry under Attack

Thomas became a bachelor (1252) and Humbert the master general (1254) when the secular clergy at Paris intensified their attack on the friars (part of the campaign of the diocesan clergy). Having no clear understanding of the new mendicant way of life, the clergy confused friars with monks and objected to their preaching, teaching, and care for souls. Resenting the popularity of the mendicant professors, the secular masters at Paris disliked the independence of the friars, their appeals for papal dispensations and privileges, and their indifference to the local concerns of the Parisian clerics. They were intent on training their men for the wider apostolate of reviving Christendom.

Dominicans were especially vulnerable because they held two chairs of theology. The Order's policy of advancing bachelors to graduation as soon as the regent master had completed his two-year period of obligatory regency gave their teaching a freshness that the long-tenured secular masters could not attain.

Dominicans discussed urgent questions of the day with dynamic comprehension, offering balanced and moderate solutions. Men like Robert Kilwardby, Remigio de Girolami, Peter of Tarentaise, Bernard of Trilia, and Richard of Knapwell, to say nothing of Albert and Thomas, produced a volume of writings that surpassed the slender production of the seculars.

By the fall of 1255, feeling against the friars had reached such a pitch at Paris that St. Jacques priory was virtually under siege. Mud, stones, garbage, and insults rained on friars who ventured out. The University refused to permit Thomas to graduate as master. However, Alexander IV licensed him to teach. When Thomas gave his inaugural lecture in 1256 his audience had to be protected by the soldiers of Louis IX.

After hearing Albert the Great's reply to William of St. Amour's book, *The Perils of the Latter Times* (a vicious attack on the friars), the Pope condemned it and banished the author and his lieutenants from Paris. Meanwhile Thomas and Bonaventure replied pointedly to the *Perils*. With William in exile, the conflict now died down. Ten years later Gerard of Abbeville, an ardent disciple of William, renewed it. Thomas, who had left Paris to teach in Italy in 1259, returned in 1269 and penned several works defending the mendicant Orders.

How serious the danger had been for the friars was seen when many bishops came to the 1274 Council of Lyons, petitioning the abolition of all the friar Orders. It suppressed the minor ones, left the fate of the Carmelites and Augustinians in balance, but praised the Franciscans and Dominicans.

Attacks on the teaching of Thomas soon after his death moved the Order quickly toward official acceptance of his teaching. It became a link in Dominican unity. The first attack came in 1277, when Bishop Stephen Tempier of Paris and Archbishop Robert Kilwardby of Canterbury (former English provincial) included theses of Thomas in lists of condemned propositions. Unlike Archbishop Kilwardby, Albert the Great, even though he differed with Thomas on some points, traveled from Cologne to Paris to speak for his former disciple. The next year, the general chapter sent two men to England to punish scholars who were disparaging the writings of Thomas. Both in France and England disciples defended the teaching of Thomas with voice and pen. The 1279 general chapter moved positively to protect his reputation and system of thought; the one in 1286 commanded the friars to promote and defend the doctrine of Thomas, "at least as an opinion." Those who did not accept it were not to attack it. The 1313 chapter capped the triumph of Thomas when it called his doctrine "sounder and more common". Long before that, friars who had studied in Paris had carried his books back to their provinces and were expounding and developing his doctrine. They compiled epitomes, concordances, commentaries, and indices to facilitate the penetration of his thought.

Dominican Writers

Dominicans were interested chiefly in biblical and theological studies, but their conviction that truth has many faces and may be taught in many ways led them down other paths as well. Over the centuries more than 5,000 writers produced thousands of volumes. We can give but a slender sampling of those written in the thirteenth century. Works in theology, Scripture, and philosophy were the most numerous. Many friars commented on the books of the Bible; Hugh of St. Cher expounded all of them. Teams of friars at Paris produced several concordances of the Scriptures and corrected the Vulgate version. Albert the Great, a universal genius, wrote books on animals, vegetables, minerals, botany, an encyclopedic commentary on Aristotle's philosophy, and works in theology and Scripture.

In pastoral theology, history, and other fields, Dominican writers compiled reference books, summas, epitomes, and manuals. The most helpful was the large handbook Raymond of Penyafort wrote for confessors, though scholars and preachers used it also. The best known is the *Speculum maius,* a large encyclopedic work in which Vincent of Beauvais stocked lore from many fields. Preachers collected sermons and sermon materials and published saints' lives. James of Voragine's collection of lives, the *Golden Legend,* is still being read. Some writers penned guidebooks for the laity. Laurence of Orleans wrote a book on the virtues and vices, the *Somme le Roi,* a medieval best seller, for Philip III of France. Dominican history writing began when Jordan of Saxony wrote an account of Dominic's life and the early days of the Order, a precious source for historians. Bernard Gui devoted himself to the history of the Order, while other friars recounted the story of a nation, city or prominent person. Theodoric Borgognoni of Lucca, a surgeon's son and a surgeon himself, published a manual of surgery. Moneta of Cremona, Bernard Gui, and Nicholas Eymeric, inquisitors themselves, prepared guidebooks for their colleagues. Thomas of Cantimprè, besides saints' lives, compiled the *De natura rerum*, one of the first encyclopedias of the natural sciences. The *Catholicon* of John Balbus of Genoa, written in 1286, was the first medieval dictionary. It dealt with the grammar, rhetoric, prosody, and orthography of late classical and medieval Latin.

The Preaching Ministry

The Order's ministries, especially its preaching and foreign missions, came to full bloom during the generalates of John of Wildeshausen and Humbert of Romans. The scarcity of able preachers and good preaching led Dominic to found his Order; preaching was the goal he set for it in the Constitutions: "...our Order was founded from the beginning for preaching and the salvation of men." Its name, "Order of Preachers", summarizes its nature and function, and presents a challenge.

Dominic structured the life of the Order and developed many innovations with preaching in view. He introduced a kind and quality of education that prepared men for preaching, abandoned manual labor, granted extensive power to dispense to superiors, prohibited undertaking parishes, coupled contemplation and ministry, and insisted on mendicant poverty in order to place at the service of the Church a self-perpetuating body of trained preachers. In the Constitutions Dominic instructed preachers to "go forth as men who seek their own salvation and that of others," living "as men of the Gospel," who, following in the footsteps of their Savior, "speak with or about God among themselves and others." To exemplify a Christlike and apostolic life, preachers were to go on foot and carry no money; nor were they to beg while preaching. Only mature and well prepared men were to be sent out.

The life and career of William Peyrault illustrates all that the Constitutions expected of a preacher. Trained in the schools of the Order in its early days, his preaching and writing demonstrate in an outstanding manner the effectiveness of Dominic's ideal. Contemporaries spoke of his high character, virtuous life, and selfless zeal: "In keeping with his religious profession, he evangelized by word, pen, and example; even in death he did not cease preaching." Surprisingly, he never became a preacher general; nor did he study at Paris or teach. His career spanned most of the century. Born before 1200, he entered the Order in the 1230's and died in the early 1270's. All the great Dominicans of the century were his contemporaries: Reginald, Bl. Diana and Bl. Cecilia, Jordan, Raymond, Humbert, Albert, Thomas, John of Vercelli. Peyrault preached for many years. Every Lent he went into the deep valleys of the Burgundian Alps, preaching and hearing confessions until late in the day. Three times he published his sermons, numbering about 500. Four other important works came from his pen, especially the *Summa of Virtues and Vices*, a comprehensive theological treatment of inestimable value to preachers, as its popularity attests. We know the names of many who matched William's record, but others, who must have preached as much, remain anonymous.

The Order appointed experienced preachers to the office of preacher general. To qualify for this position, a friar had to have a firm theological knowledge, and must have preached successfully in a variety of places and under many circumstances. To keep his office, he had to preach often, be ready for special sermons, and attend the provincial chapter. Only one preacher general was to be assigned to a priory, though when friars began to consider the position an honor rather than a function an excessive number were appointed.

Stephen of Bourbon exemplifies the career of an outstanding preacher general. He lived at the priory of Lyons when Humbert of Romans was its prior, and William Peyrault and Peter of Tarentaise (theologian, archbishop of Lyons and pope) were members of the community. For forty years, Stephen preached extensively throughout France, especially in the southeast and Burgundy. He was one of the best known figures in the country and knew most of his famous contemporaries. When old, he prepared a handbook of materials for preachers, recording the anecdotes and experience which had lent color to his own sermons.

Stephen's book is only one of the hundreds of preaching aids prepared by Dominicans. They gathered materials, collected sermons and outlines, compiled works of reference, discussed preaching methods, and compiled handbooks of anecdotes and other source material. The encyclopedic *Speculum maius* of Vincent of Beauvais was a gold mine for preachers. The fourteenth-century *Summa praedicantium* of the English Dominican John of Bromyard is a large reservoir of preaching lore—theological, historical, and illustrative. Other books in the arsenal of the preacher were biblical glossaries, commentaries, and concordances, the *Decretals of Gregory IX*, chronicles, histories, lives of the saints, and the works of the Fathers. These books were readily available in the well-stocked Dominican libraries. Speaking from experience, Stephen of Bourbon refers to the effectiveness of examples:

> *We have learned by much long experience that preachers who use plenty of examples have preached more graciously and gathered more fruit. Indeed, examples are useful for all men, all states of life, for illustrating all kinds of material. They help to turn people from evil and to inculcate, acquire, and promote every good. They can be employed in all times and places, in all kinds of sermons and exhortations.*

Medieval preachers used legends, referred to natural phenomena, cited historical events and scientific facts, quoted from saints' lives, and drew on personal experience.

To speak the word "friar" is to cause the image of a wandering preacher to flash across the minds of many people. They picture him walking down roads and highways, stopping to preach at crossroads, in the market places and on street corners. There was much outdoor preaching in those days, especially in warm climates. Preaching crosses stood at crossroads, in cemeteries and churchyards. We know that the priories of Brecon, Bristol, London, Norwich, and Herford in England had such crosses. The last two still stand.

Outside preaching was not the norm; usually the friars preached in their own chapels or in parish churches, when these were open to them.

As soon as the friars increased in number, the Order organized its preaching ministry. Each priory worked and begged alms within a definite territory assigned to it. Friars visited this area regularly, especially during Advent and Lent. They preached mostly in cities and towns and went to country villages outside great liturgical seasons. Siger of Lille preached so successfully in his native city during the 1230's, even before a priory stood there, that he became spiritual director of Margaret of Ypres and a group of women who formed around her. Priories subdivided their territory and entrusted each subdivision, called a "limit," to an experienced preacher, a "limiter," to use the name made famous or infamous, by Chaucer's friar.

There was a Friar, a wanton one and merry,
A Limiter, a very festive fellow.

In the fifteenth century, the priory of Langres had eight major and eight minor limits. One of them included fifty-seven parishes. When he worked in an outlying district, a friar stayed for days at a time. In the fifteenth century, the friars maintained small preaching houses in which the friars could stay, even for weeks.

When the mendicants realized that parish priests were unwilling to let them preach in the churches (after 1240), they built priory churches with roomy, hall-like naves to accommodate large congregations. To reap greater fruit from their preaching, and the confessions that often followed it, the friars gained permission from the Church to impart indulgences, absolve from reserved sins, hold services during interdicts, and bury the faithful in their churches. To draw people to their sermons, they promoted their Third Orders, founded confraternities honoring

Jesus, Mary, and Dominic, and developed new devotions. The traditional processions on the four Sundays of the month venerating Mary, the Holy Name, the Blessed Sacrament, and St. Dominic, each originally a confraternity obligation, illustrate these devotions. During the processions and confraternity meetings popular hymns, especially Marian, were sung. Often after the *Hail Holy Queen* was chanted at the end of Compline, the people stayed to sing hymns in Mary's honor. When the friars shortened their liturgical services to permit more time for sermons, parish priests complained, probably considering the move an unfair tactic.

Matthew Paris, an English Benedictine monk, who resented the friars, gives unintentional witness to their zeal when he grumbled that their "urgent preachings," defrauded the "legitimate Orders," i.e., canons and monks, of their customary offerings. He tells how the friars "poor indeed in food and clothing, ... went through the cities, villages, and boroughs preaching the word of the Gospel ... they went shod in aid of the Gospel, slept clothed, used mats for their beds and sacks for pillows on which they lay their heads."

Dominicans preached often. Sermons delivered to the congregations in priory churches often averaged 240 to 250 a year. The friars preached morning and evening, on Sundays and feastdays, on every day of Lent, on the vigils of Christmas and Pentecost, on Rogation Days and the Saturdays of Ember weeks and during the octaves of Easter and Pentecost. Preachers of penance like John of Vincenza, Vincent Ferrer, Manfred of Vercelli, and Savonarola are noted for the frequency and power of their preaching. Vincent Ferrer preached daily for forty years, often two or three times.

An impressive number of Dominicans filled both the professor's chair and the preacher's pulpit, men like Albert and Thomas. An important duty of professors in the Order's schools and at the universities was to preach on days reserved to them. Vincent Ferrer had been a successful teacher and writer before he began the preaching tours that rank him among the Church's great evangelists.

Sermons covered the whole range of Christian doctrine and

practice. "Totally dedicated to the preaching of the word of God," existing "to stamp out heresy, uproot vice, teach the faith and train men in good morals," Dominicans gave their sermons a strong, evangelical content, often embedded in layers of illustrative material. They avoided bare exhortation.

When Dominic founded the Order of Preachers, he enabled bishops, by delegating the friars, to carry out a recommendation of Lateran Council IV. The Holy Father, too, found the friars important auxiliaries in executing his plans and often entrusted special preaching assignments to them. Any time a pope declared a crusade, he commissioned the friars to proclaim it. Albert the Great was one of the many who preached the Cross. When Lyons Council II (1274) sought to remedy the blasphemy and cursing that were prevalent, it ordered that the faithful should reverence the name of Jesus "by bending the knee of their hearts and showing this by bowing the head." After the Council, Gregory X commissioned the Dominicans to preach the Holy Name. From these roots, at a later date, sprang the Holy Name Confraternity, which became such a power in drawing men to the sacraments in twentieth-century America. In the fourteenth century, John XXII deputed all the mendicants to preach against gambling.

Dominic rendered a great service to the faithful when he opened the doors of preaching for his Order. This becomes clear when we review the little preaching that was done and the sparse amount of preaching material produced during the centuries that stretch from the age of the great Fathers to the days of Dominic. Before the thirteenth century reached mid-point, the great scarcity of preachers that had led to the foundation of the Order of Preachers had vanished. The door Dominic opened for it remained open and the other Orders and priests marched through too. He cut the cords that had checked priests other than pastors from proclaiming the word of God. In the thirteenth century Franciscans preached as often and produced as much sermon material as Dominicans.

Preaching involved Dominicans in many related activities. Following his sermon, the preacher usually stepped into the confessional. Common people, aristocrats, kings, and sometimes popes chose a friar as confessor. The disciples of Dominic guided the English royal house until the Plantagenet line came to its sad end under Richard II. Other friars acted as counsellors, legates, ambassadors, arbitrators, executors of wills, visitators of churches and monasteries, and peacemakers. Geoffrey of Beaulieu was confessor of St. Louis IX of France. He went with him on his crusade of Tunis and wrote his biography. In 1239 the King sent Friar James and Andrew of Longjumeau to Constantinople to bring the Crown of Thorns, a gift of Baldwin II, to Paris. Louis built the jewel-like Sainte Chapelle to house the relic.

Honorius III and Gregory IX thought so well of the prudence and tact of Bl. Guala of Bergamo that they sent him on a number of difficult affairs, among them a mission as peacemaker in Lombardy. A very early peace effort involving Dominicans was the preaching campaign of 1233, known as the Alleluia. A freelance preacher inaugurated the movement, proclaiming peace, expiation, and self-renunciation. He sought to unite the factions and heal the feuds which kept Lombardy at the boiling point. Dominicans joined the campaign and John of Vicenza became its leader. Franciscans too came into action. Towns became reconciled. Some of them entrusted the revision of their statutes to John; Vicenza and Verona appointed him podestà. Following much preliminary preaching and arbitration, he attempted to introduce a general peace, preaching an open air sermon from a high platform at Paquara, August 28, 1233. Chroniclers claim that more than 400,000 people were present. But the peace John made was as meteoric as his own career. The year 1233 saw his rise, climb to power, loss of influence, and the collapse of the peace movement. It shared the fate of similar efforts in Italy before and after John. Perhaps personal ambition contributed to his failure.

In response to the works of the friars, the faithful invited them to found priories, helped them construct their buildings, gave them alms and chose burial in their churches. Louis IX was a munificent friend of the Order. He put up buildings for St. Jacques, founded the Priories of Caen and Compiègne, and encouraged the one at Evreux. English kings often sent money and supplies to the Dominicans, and, in the fourteenth century, founded and built the house at King's, Langley and the nuns' monastery at Dartford.

Dominican and Franciscan Rivalry

An unfortunate by-product of Dominican success was rivalry with the Franciscans. Brothers in spirit and ministry, the sons of Dominic and Francis clashed over theological opinions, the making of foundations, sources of alms and benefactions, and recruits. To attract vocations, each side pointed to its own apostolicity, claiming closer imitation of the Twelve than its rival. Like the Apostles in their preaching and poverty, they were unlike them in the ambition and self-seeking they sometimes displayed. The two Orders are so much alike—Dominicans imitate Christ the Preacher who was poor, while Franciscans follow Christ the Poor Man who preached the Good News—that they could not help clashing from time to time. From the quarrels came mutual respect and love. The century-old custom of having Dominicans officiate at their liturgy on the feastday of Francis, and Franciscans on the feast of Dominic is the symbol of this deeper harmony.

The Inquisition

Gregory IX, who organized the medieval inquisition in 1231, soon enlisted Dominicans as inquisitors. They were not the only inquisitors. Immediately appointed by their provincials, these friars, when active, were largely outside the Order's control. They engaged in work that Humbert listed as odious, since it turned people away from the Order and its ministry. Yet, as mistaken as the inquisition is now seen to be, its basic intention of defending the faith and reclaiming the heretic, was in keeping with the Order's vocation to proclaim God's word and preserve it from adulteration. The inquisition was never active in some countries (England was one of them) and not equally active in all places or all times. Early in its life (1242) Albigenses, the heretics Dominic worked among, murdered Bl. William Arnault, inquisitor in Toulouse, two companions, and several diocesan priests at Avignonet. The more noted martyr, St. Peter of Verona, and his cooperator brother companion were ambushed and killed by heretics in northern Italy in 1252. In the fourteenth century, the inquisition at Avignon imprisoned Thomas Waleys, an English Dominican, for daring to attack the erroneous opinions about the beatific vision that John XXII held as a private theologian. When the inquisitors brought another charge against Thomas, the Pope held him in the papal jail for eleven years. The most noted victims of the inquisition in medieval times were the Knights Templars, St. Joan of Arc, and Savonarola, with his two companions. These cases were unworthily motivated. Dominicans were involved in the first, reluctantly cooperated in the second, and were victims in the third.

The Last Eighteen Years

The first five generals who followed Dominic had a combined tenure of sixty-two years; the next five governed for eighteen, from 1285 to 1303. The election of Munio of Zamora in 1285 signalled the passing of the Order's great age. Some have called it golden, but this glowing description betrays reality. Even in its earliest and best days, the Order had to pursue apostate and fugitive brethren, imprison incorrigible friars, punish ambition and imprudent zeal, settle squabbles between priories and provinces, and inflict penances on a hoard of individual friars. Yet it was a time of great achievement. It was coming to an end when Munio was elected; events were becoming too strong for men to control. Tendencies began to appear which the best insight, most suitable plans, and finest character were unable to check. Economic recession, wars, and natural disasters were waiting in the wings as Munio took office. His choice seemed to promise years of capable administration and a continuance of achievement. He himself was determined to uphold discipline and maintain morale at its peak. General chapters held under his presidency punished breaches of poverty, appetite for honors and titles, and gossip that ran to slander and calumny.

Munio himself fell victim to false rumors. The 1287 chapter inflicted heavy penances on a number of friars for spreading unproved charges against him. Nevertheless, Nicholas IV deposed him in 1291. The pope fired the opening gun at Munio when he granted two Dominican cardinals wide authority "to order, arrange, correct, reform, and do sundry other things that they shall before God deem appropriate for the advance of the Order." Delegated by the cardinals, four friars carried their letters and instructions to the 1290 chapter. The diffinitors were to persuade the general to resign; should he prove reluctant they were to depose him. After examining his conduct, they did the opposite, commending him. When the four friars high-handedly deposed Munio, the chapter appealed to the Holy See and commanded the Order to pray daily to the Blessed Mother during their masses, matins, and vespers. Nicholas IV remained adamant. He ordered Munio to resign at the next chapter, in 1291, and notified the diffinitors that the general's authority would expire when the chapter began. Munio did not resign, and the papal letter never reached its destination. Thereupon Nicholas removed him. The unfortunate general retired to his native Spain.

In 1294 Munio was elected to the episcopate of Palencia. Pope Celestine V confirmed him in the post, but before the end of the year enemies apparently began to sabotage him again. Under Boniface VIII he was charged, investigated, and cleared. But he had had enough. With papal consent he resigned his bishopric and went to Rome to live at Santa Sabina. There he died in 1300 and was buried under the church floor. A magnificent mosaic, executed by a Dominican co-operator brother, decorates the marble slab that perpetuates his memory.

Munio seems to have been caught in a mesh of papal politics involving the Kingdom of Aragon, a part of his jurisdiction when he was provincial of Spain. Though the reasons for the Dominican opposition to him are not known, they seem to be linked with the attempts of the chapters he presided over to remove abuses. The 1290 chapter emphasized the common life and counteracted a growing desire for security, manifested in the acquisition of houses, mills, and other sources of fixed revenue. Also, the multiplication of preachers general during the 1280's, when professors, priors, and former provincials were elevated to the office, testifies to inordinate ambition. It became a reward for services rather than the entrusting of a function.

Munio of Zamora organized an important arm of Dominican action and influence when he promulgated a Rule for the Third Order. Perhaps this was the most lasting act of his regime. The Franciscan and Dominican Third Orders grew from the twelfth-century, lay, penitential movement. Brothers and Sisters of Penance were not affiliated to any Order but sought spiritual guidance from nearby priests. When Dominican or Franciscan priories were founded, they grouped around them, depending on their proximity to one or the other. Though Munio's Rule did not receive explicit papal approbation until 1405, Honorius IV tacitly approved it when he granted privileges to the Brothers and Sisters of Penance of St. Dominic in 1286.

The Order's first century (1215-1303) witnessed the flowering of its ministry, the formation of its school system, the eminence of its scholarship, and the leadership of an exceptional number of able masters general who gave every sign of listening to the Spirit. Under their fearless leadership, friars developed apostolates as preachers, missionaries, and confessors. They served as bishops, inquisitors, ambassadors, legates, mediators, and arbitrators, attended general councils and worked for the union of the eastern and western Churches. The holiness displayed by these early Dominicans illustrates that the tension caused by the Order's thrust towards both contemplation and ministry can be harmonized, and most perfectly so at the summit of excellence. It is an excellence resulting from conformity to Christ the Preacher; the poor, chaste, and obedient God-man who proclaimed the Good News of salvation. Dominican men and women, prayerfully pondering and experiencing the word of God, both Incarnate and written, become like Christ, contemplative apostles working for the Kingdom of God and the salvation of men.

Many reasons explain the glory of the Order's first century. Father Dominic, the Founder, had listened to the Spirit and the Church. Given to the Church by the Spirit, his Order responded to her vital needs and those of society. The Order of Preachers was the first to demonstrate strikingly the ministerial potentialities of the religious life. Until Dominic, the active ministry had been an appendage, not an integral part, of the religious life. He breached the wall through which later Founders marched with their Orders. As its first century ended, the Order began to weaken, but so did the Church and Western Christendom. The conflicts of Boniface VIII with Philip of France and Edward of England, kings of new national states, heralded a new age, an age made great by mystics and saints but weak by disaster, confusion and schism. The Order shared both the greatness and the weakness.

CHAPTER III

THE MISSIONS TO 1500

Dominican missions sprang naturally from the Order's soil and drew nourishment from the Founder's spirit. Though frustrated in his own burning ambition to evangelize unbelievers— he had hungered for the conversion of the Cumans in the East, the Moors in his homeland, and the pagans of the North—Dominic passed the torch to his sons.

The Missionaries

Missionaries came from all over the Order. As a rule, only volunteers were sent and appear to have been well qualified and educated. Often chroniclers remark that a missionary was "trained in letters," "sufficiently instructed in theology." Franco of Perugia, for example, had been bachelor of the *Sentences* before going to the East as a missionary.

Though the *Lives of the Brethren* was written to console the brethren, help them advance in the spiritual life, and show them "how carefully Providence has befriended our Order," it contains valuable illustrations of the spirit of the early generation of friars. It reports several incidents that show the missionary zeal of the early Dominicans. It notes that when Jordan of Saxony asked the brethren who were present for the general chapter, probably at Paris in 1230, for volunteers for the Holy Land, there was scarcely a person who did not beg with tear-filled eyes "to be sent to that land which the Lord's Blood had hallowed." Jordan's concern for the missions carried him on an inspection tour of the province of the Holy Land. He died on his return journey when his ship foundered off the coast of Palestine.

The 1255 and 1256 encyclicals of Humbert of Romans testify to the continuance of enthusiasm for the missions and to Humbert's own zeal. His request for volunteers got such a response that all who came forward could not be accepted. He had to write in 1256 urging those whose services could not be used at once to be patient. Of course, such zeal did not remain at fever pitch. Humbert shrewdly observed that two things keep men from volunteering for the missions, "love of one's own country and ignorance of languages."

To encourage missionaries, the Order made concessions to the mission provinces of Greece and the Holy Land, and to the Congregation of Pilgrim Friars, founded in 1300 for work in eastern Europe and Asia. Not taxed for common endeavors, they might recruit missionaries anywhere and were not subject to levies on their own manpower. However, they were obliged to respect the membership of each other.

In his book on the officers of the Order, Humbert reminds the master general of his duty to promote the missions. As general, Humbert had exemplified what he had written. Not only did he seek volunteers, but, to encourage them, reported their successes to the Order. His 1256 encyclical gives a glowing account of their work in the Near East.

Raymond of Penyafort showed zeal for the missions both before and after his term as general. While still penitentiary at the papal court, he replied in detail to a series of questions the Dominican and Franciscan missionaries in Tunis had sent to him. After he had retired to Spain, following his resignation from the generalate, Raymond lifted the veil which usually hides the day-by-day work of the missionaries when John of Wildeshausen asked him for a report on the Spanish and African missions. Dominicans were working among the many Christian soldiers in the pay of the Arabs, reconciling apostates from the faith and instructing Christian slaves who were descendants of the pre-Arab population of northern Africa and ignorant of any language but Arabic. Others who were on the verge of apostasy because of poverty or the blandishments of the Moors, they strengthened. They confirmed in the faith, and sometimes liberated, Christian prisoners. Especially in Murcia, many Arabs, even some prominent men, had accepted Christianity. The friars were also answering Moors and apostates who charged that Christians were idolators because they venerated statues and images. It was Raymond's opinion that the field was ripe for more conversions, provided missionaries would come.

The Study of Native Languages

In Spain, Raymond became the foremost promoter of the missions. With his encouragement, his province opened a school of Arabic studies at Tunis in 1250. For varying periods it maintained other schools for Oriental languages at Barcelona, Valencia, Xativa, and Murcia. Well into the next century, the general chapters encouraged study of eastern languages, as did the general council of Vienne in 1312. The 1333 general chapter required the vicar of the Pilgrim Friars to appoint language teachers at Kaffa and Pera in Constantinople to prepare for an influx of new missionaries who were expected in response to John XXII's appeal for fifty volunteers.

That Raymond intended something more than linguistic study at these schools is demonstrated by his request to Thomas Aquinas, asking him to write something on the doctrines of faith to help prepare missionaries for their work among unbelievers. Though Thomas had additional purposes in mind when he wrote it, he produced his *Summa contra Gentiles* in reply.

Probably most missionaries learned the native tongues in the field. Writing to Gregory IX in 1236, Provincial Philip noted how zealously the members of the province of the Holy Land were studying the Oriental languages. Three years earlier, when two Dominicans and two Franciscans came as papal emissaries to the Greek Emperor at Nicea, Dominicans of Constantinople provided an interpreter who spoke Greek fluently and had studied the Greek fathers. With pardonable pride, Franco of Perugia, first vicar of the Pilgrim Friars, boasted of his own linguistic prowess: "I preached within a year after I began to study the barbarian tongue. By the grace of God I preach to the people, hear confessions, and also translate writings from the Latin." Louis of Tabriz was appointed director of St. Anthony parish at Pera in 1403 because he was able to preach to the inhabitants, merchants, pilgrims, and travelers who passed through the city in Greek, Latin, Persian, Tartar, and Armenian.

Missionary Authors

The Order made an effort to provide books for the missionaries. The Master General had a duty, Humbert of Romans reminded him, to provide "treatises exposing the errors of these people, so that the friars can drill themselves in them." Like the preachers, the missionaries wrote books to help their fellows. They were of two kinds. The first were polemical works that prepared men for discussion with Dissidents, Jews, Moors, and pagans. Other books, originating mostly in the East, described the experiences of the missionaries or recorded the beliefs and practices of Moslems. A few examples will illustrate this activity.

Raymond Martin, a pioneer orientalist in Spain, restricted his *Halter of the Jews* (*Capistrum Judaeorum*) to Jewish controversy, but directed his *Dagger of the Faith* (*Pugio Fidei*) toward both Jews and Moslems. He also compiled an Arabic dictionary. Ricoldo of Montecroce, who worked in Mesopotamia and Syria, in his *Itinerary* enriched Western thought with a wealth of ethnological and religious details about Tartars, Curds, Sabei, Jacobites, Nestorians, and Moslems. He also wrote a *Refutation of the Koran.* His five letters sent after the fall of Acre in 1291 are a beautiful and unforgettable tribute to Dominican mission idealism. The tolerance and conciliation William of Tripoli exhibits in his study of Islam explains why he could boast that he had baptized more than 1,000 Moslems. Burchard of Monte Zion's description of the *Holy Land,* a mine of information, was for three centuries the classical manual of Palestinian and Near-Eastern topography. The *Itineraries* of Felix Fabri, who went as a pilgrim twice to the Near East in the late fifteenth century, describe the Holy Land for "stay-at-homes" rather than missionaries. The crusading treatises of

William Adam and Raymond Stephen were not missionary books but aimed to further "the business of the Cross."

The Mission Fields

The friars preferred some mission fields over others. French and Italian Dominicans sought the Near East and Asia; French friars were in the majority in thirteenth-century Palestine; Italians were in the forefront in fourteenth-century Mesopotamia and Persia. An occasional English, German, or Spanish friar found his way to the East. After 1300, wanderlust or thirst for adventure rather than zeal induced some friars to join the Pilgrim Friars. The frontier provinces—Scandinavia, Germany, Poland, Hungary, Greece, and Palestine had a first duty to mission territory inside their limits. But from these springboards their friars and volunteers from other provinces jumped into mission lands.

The efforts of the Spanish, Scandinavian, and Hungarian provinces reflect the zeal of Dominic. He had sent the first men to Spain and Scandinavia; during his last days, friars assigned by the second general chapter were traveling to Poland and Hungary. In 1225 contingents were en route to Greece and the Holy Land, areas the 1221 chapter had designated as future provinces.

Spanish Dominicans labored among Jews and Moors at home, across their southern borders in the Peninsula, and in Africa. They entered Morocco before 1225 and Tunis before 1230.

Alexander IV spurred renewed interest in the Tunisian mission, when he called for Dominican and Franciscan volunteers in 1254 and 1258. On his deathbed King Louis IX singled out Andrew Longjumeau, who had preached in Tunis, as best fitted to head the Tunisian preaching apostolate. The crusade of Louis temporarily halted missionary work, but the subsequent treaty and commercial agreements of Italian cities with Tunis created more favorable conditions for evangelization. However, it was still greatly restricted. Apparently on the advice of Raymond of Penyafort, in 1242, James I of Aragon prescribed Jewish and Moorish attendance at sermons preached by bishops and friars. A similar policy was resumed in 1263 at the urging of Pablo Christiani, a Dominican convert Jew.

In southern Italy the Order was entrusted with preaching to the Saracen soldiers in the armies of Frederick II in 1233.

The Scandinavian Dominicans not only worked to complete the Christianization of their own lands but pushed eastward to the pagans surrounding the Baltic Sea. They entered Finland in the wake of the Swedish conquests there in 1239. Ten years later they placed a priory in Abo. It was still the only religious house in Finland more than 150 years later. The pope appointed Dominicans to preach in central Europe, enlist recruits, and gather funds for the Finnish crusade of the Teutonic Knights. The treaty with the Finns provided for their conversion. The laborious work of really converting the natives involved the cooperation of bishops, parish priests, and friars. Dominicans were appointed to three of the four bishoprics established. The Order was so influential that Finnish dioceses adopted its liturgy.

Polish friars toiled among the Russian Orthodox in Kiev. There Hyacinth, who had introduced the Order to Poland, had founded a priory in 1222. Unfortunately, the history of the priories founded in Russia in the 1250's is unknown. Hyacinth established a strategic point for the evangelization of Prussians, Lithuanians, and Latvians when he opened a house at Gdansk (Danzig). The Polish and German provinces played a predominant role in organizing the church of Lithuania, following the conversion of King Mindowe. His untimely death (and perhaps apostasy in 1235) terminated this missionary attempt for a century.

Following an initial setback, Hungarian friars made so much progress in converting the Cumans that Friar Theodore was named their bishop in 1227, the first Dominican to enter the hierarchy. The Tartar invasions of 1241 overwhelmed the Cuman areas and Hungary, killing ninety friars and burning down two priories. The Cumans were scattered, but drifted back after the invasions. Mission work began again. In 1256 Humbert of Romans spoke of "a great multitude of Cumans" that had been converted, but, for the most part, work among them was discouraging. In 1339, nearly 100 years later, most of the Cumans were still pagan.

The Hungarian provincial, John of Wildeshausen, took part

in unsuccessful attempts to reunite the Bulgarians to Rome. His versatility is illustrated by his ability to speak five languages and by the offices he held. In turn he became bishop of Bosnia (resigning later), provincial of Lombardy, and master general.

The most romantic and difficult exploit of the Hungarian Dominicans was their search for the remnants of their people who had remained in the primitive homeland on the middle Volga River, called Greater Hungary. The friars read in chronicles how part of the clan had migrated and part stayed behind, "sunk in the error of infidelity." They knew Greater Hungary was in the East, but none could say where. From 1232 to 1237 four contingents set out to search for it. After great hardship, only Friar Julian reached Greater Hungary. Its people received him royally; when he returned a second time in 1237, he found that the Tartars had submerged them and mission work was impossible. Julian's reports describing the search are epic in the sheer heroism they record and valuable for the fresh knowledge of Russia and the Tartars they preserve.

The Order also worked in Albania, where it founded some priories. Thirteenth-century efforts in southern Russia are shrouded in darkness. A foundation was made at Tiflis, Georgia, before 1238. Continuing work in the Near East is illustrated by the preaching and debating of Ricoldo of Montecroce among the Jacobites, Nestorians, Jews, and Arabs in Mosul and Bagdad during a twelve-year stay in Mesopotamia. He met other Dominicans in Bagdad, where the Order had no house, in 1289.

The Order founded provinces in Greece and the Holy Land in 1228. Both were always small provinces with six or seven priories at the most and both saw their effectiveness as missionary enterprises destroyed through enemy action early in their existence. The Dominicans of the Grecian province worked among the western Christians in the Latin Empire of Constantinople, in the colonies of Venice, and among the Dissident Christians in Greece and its islands. It lost its chief priory in Constantinople when the Byzantine Empire was reestablished there in 1261, and its remaining priories, except Candia, to the onrushing Turks, who took Constantinople in 1453. The province continued in Crete until that island also fell to the Turks in 1669.

The Dominicans of the Holy Land evangelized western and Dissident Christians, Moslems, and Jews, inside their territory and eastward. After the fall of Acre in 1291, the province continued in three priories on Cyprus until the Turks captured the island in 1571. Its friars reunited several prelates of the separated churches and Rome during the generalate of Jordan of Saxony and converted many Saracens.

Probably the most lasting contribution of the friars to the union of the Greek and Latin Churches lies in the field of writing. A number of them who had personal contact with Easterners, or scholars with other sources of information, produced writings dealing with Eastern problems during the medieval centuries. At the request of Urban IV, Thomas Aquinas interrupted his composition of the *Summa contra Gentiles* to write the *Contra errores Graecorum*. In the book he examined the procession of the Holy Spirit and statements of the Greek Fathers about it.

Nicholas of Vicenza and William of Tripoli, who had done excellent work in Palestine, lost a chance for undying fame when Pope Gregory X gave them letters for the Grand Khan in central Asia and sent them in the company of the Polo brothers. After spending long years in China, Marco Polo, their nephew, returned to a fame that has never been tarnished. However, the friars turned back soon after setting out when the campaign of Sultan Bibars of Egypt frightened them.

The Asiatic Tartars and the Dominicans

Dominican contact with the Tartars was extended by a design of Innocent IV. Thinking he could contain the Moslems and perhaps facilitate their acceptance of Christianity, the Pope inaugurated a plan for an alliance with the Tartars in Asia and their conversion. In 1245, he sent four embassies, two of Dominicans and two of Franciscans, to the Tartars in southern and central Asia. Franciscans, headed by John of Plano Carpini, reached the Grand Khan in Karakorum. John's colorful account of their travels is well known. The Dominican groups contacted Tartar generals in Mesopotamia. Simon of St. Quentin described the experiences of one of the Dominican bands. It is incorporated into the

Speculum maius of Vincent of Beauvais but does not rival the Franciscan report. Andrew of Longjumeau, who had headed one of the groups, had hardly returned when Louis IX sent him back to the Tartars. He reached the court at Karakorum.

Innocent's grand plan came to nothing. Though doing credit to his missionary zeal, it presumed that the political situation and aims of Asia matched those of Europe. Even had the objectives of the Tartars and Innocent been in harmony, the practical obstacles to carrying them out were insurmountable. The report of St. Quentin shows that at least one of Innocent's embassies lacked diplomatic finesse when it made demands on the Tartar general as though he were a papal subject. The Dominican ambassadors were lucky to escape with their lives. However, the anger of the Tartars died down and the lengthy stay of the friars among them ended on a happier note.

Garden-variety missionaries also worked in Asia. Returning from China in 1254, the Franciscan, William Rubruk, met two contingents of Dominicans who were seeking to enter the Tartar dominions. In 1274 two Dominicans made their appearance, perhaps as interpreters, in the company of a Tartar embassy to the Council of Lyons. In the fifteenth century, the Dominican Archbishop in eastern Armenia, John of Sultania, knew Tamerlane, the Khan of the Tartars, and led an embassy to Europe for him.

The Congregation of Pilgrim Friars

The missions of the Order lagged for a time after the Saracens took Acre in 1291 and closed the trade routes originating in Palestine. The friars could not travel eastward and were forced off the mainland to footholds on Cyprus. However, a new organization rallied the Order's eastern missionaries. Founded between 1300 and 1304, the Society of Friars Travelling for the Sake of Christ among the Gentiles, later called the Congregation of Pilgrim Friars, began to work from outposts on the shifting frontiers between Christendom, Islam, and paganism. Governed by a vicar general under statutes given by Master General Berengar of Landorra, the Pilgrims were more flexible than a province. They had no fixed territory and recruited their men from the rest of the Order. The Congregation reached the peak of its activities about 1330, when it had missions at Trebizond and Chios, at two points in Turkey, in Georgia, Turkestan, Persia, and India. The Pilgrims tried in vain to enter China. Before they were founded, Nicholas of Pistoia started to China with the Franciscan, John of Montecorvino, but died while preaching in India. Montecorvino reached Pekin, where he established a successful mission. One of the Pilgrims, Jordan of Catalani, founded a mission at Quilon in India, becoming its first bishop.

After Poland conquered Red Russia in 1349, Polish friars founded priories in that area, but a quarter of a century later turned them over to the Pilgrim Friars.

The Black Death destroyed all but three of the missions of the Pilgrims, Pera, Kaffa, and Trebrizond. It forced the 1363 general chapter to incorporate these houses into the province of Greece. Restored in 1373, the Pilgrims evangelized in Russia, Poland, Lithuania, and the Danubian principalities of Moldavia, Wallachia, and Ruthenia. The Congregation was suppressed a second time (1456-1464) following the fall of Constantinople. Then restored to life, it endured until 1857 (from 1603 under the name Congregation of the Orient and of Constantinople). At that time the remaining houses were incorporated into the province of Piedmont. At the house in the Pera-Galata, suburb of Istanbul, the Piedmontese Dominicans are presently engaged in Islamic studies.

The Unifying Friars of St. Gregory

Greater Armenia (on the Black Sea in Iran) was one of the areas evangelized by the Pilgrim Friars. They supplied the bishops of the ecclesiastical province of Sultania in western Persia, erected by John XXII in 1318. Their most striking success was the conversion of the eastern monks of Qrna in 1330. Under Abbot John Qrna adopted the Dominican liturgy, Constitutions (minus their perpetual abstinence and absolute poverty), and the habit of the cooperator brothers (white tunic with black scapular and hood). Other monasteries soon joined Qrna. With Dominican guidance, Abbot John then formed the Unifying

Friars of St. Gregory the Illuminator. Their aim was to work for the union of the Armenian and Latin Churches by preaching, teaching, and writing. Aided by Dominican translators, especially James Targman (the Translator), the Armenian friars translated the Dominican Constitutions and liturgical texts and many Western theological works, notably those of Thomas Aquinas. When Innocent VI approved the Unifiers in 1356, he placed them under the care and jurisdiction of the Dominican master general. Their monasteries stood in Armenia, Georgia, and Crimea.

During the last twenty-five years of the century, the Unifiers are said to have enrolled 700 members, living in fifty monasteries. If these figures are realistic, they soon dropped after 1381 when zealous nationalists opposed the Unifiers, and the new Tartar incursions began. When the Dominicans mitigated their perpetual abstinence and strict poverty in the second half of the fifteenth century, the distinction between them and the Unifiers began to melt away. It became customary to regard and speak of the Unifiers as Dominicans. Finally, the Order incorporated them as the province of Naxivan in 1583. Its friars continued to work in Armenia until the wars, beginning in 1750, drove them out. The last of them died at Smyrna in 1813.

The Unifying Friars of St. Gregory made an interesting attempt to serve as a bridge between the Roman and Armenian Churches and provide a well-trained native clergy. It was no fault of theirs that wars, persecution, and the ill feeling of their separated brethren stultified their effort.

Evaluation of the Missions

Dominican missionaries of the Middle Ages suffered all the handicaps and exhibit most of the flaws found in the methods of their day. Some of these were a matter of mistaken policy, such as mass or forced conversions, exemplified in Prussia where the Teutonic Knights required reception of Baptism in their treaties with the natives, employing friars to administer the Sacrament. Kings in Spain obliged Jews and Moors to attend sermons. There was also little continuity or follow-up. Ricoldo of Montecroce, during his long apostolate in Mesopotamia, established sound principles for work among Dissidents, but, after making conversions, even he hurried on to new conquests. The missionaries were plagued by distance and the hardships of travel, and a disaster could cripple an organized effort. Thus the Black Death in 1348 decimated the Pilgrim Friars. Political conditions sometimes interrupted or destroyed promising beginnings. In this way, the Tartar invasions in 1241 halted and almost put an end to the work of the Hungarian Dominicans among the Cumans. The fifteenth-century incursions of Tamerlane destroyed churches and buildings in Georgia. When he returned to Asia, the friars had to begin again. Likewise, Western missionaries misunderstood the oriental mind and failed in their appeal to the people and clergy. In Saracen lands political law and social convention made conversion difficult. Evangelization was done secretly and little record of it remains.

Dominicans gave their lives for the faith. Tartars killed ninety-four friars, among them Bl. Sadoc, their leader, and destroyed five priories in Poland and two in Hungary. Another group of Dominican martyrs suffered at Sandomir, Poland, but the time and circumstances of their death are unknown. When Acre fell in 1291, the last Dominican priory in Palestine offered thirty of its members as a holocaust. Ricoldo of Montecroce found Dominican vestments, books, breviaries, and blood-stained habits pierced by swords among the booty brought into Bagdad from Acre. A Dominican nun, the lone survivor, gave him details of the slaughter.

Bl. Anthony of Neyrot presents an interesting case. Captured by the Moors and taken to Tunis, he first apostatized, but then repented and preached Christ. The Bey had him stoned to death in 1460.

Even though the historian can point to few lasting results of the heroic self-sacrifices of the medieval Dominican missionaries, he must admit they added luster to the Church, testified to the vitality of the Order, and excited later missionaries to similar efforts. They illustrate the need to search constantly for enlightened methods of evangelization.

CHAPTER IV

THE FOURTEENTH CENTURY

In 1300 the signs that the greatness of the thirteenth century had passed could not be read with the clarity now possible. As the century advanced and witnessed a succession of conflicts, wars, and disasters, the decline became clearer. World-shaking events, each a blow to the stability and vitality of Christendom, followed one another with the speed of lightning. The quarrels between Pope Boniface VIII and King Philip the Fair of France, which had begun earlier, opened the century; the Western Schism, stretching from 1378 to 1418, during which rival popes contested the throne of Peter, closed it. In between lay the suppression of the Order of the Knights Templar, the struggle of the popes with Emperor Louis of Bavaria, and the opening of the Hundred Years War between England and France (1337). In the very middle of the century, the bubonic plague, called the Black Death, took the lives of one-third to one-half the population of Europe in two years' time. Society, Church, clergy, and Orders suffered from these disasters.

The Dominican Order still stood forth in the fullness of its strength and influence in 1300. It could hope for a future full of life and fruitful activity. Pope John XXII had high praise for it in 1317: "Endowed above other Orders with a richer grace of service, the Order of Preachers radiates a greater clarity." In 1325 John rejoiced over the "starlike splendor of this Order and the firmness of its organization for the service of God." Two years earlier he had canonized Thomas Aquinas.

Despite this glory, signs of decay were evident. Religious discipline was declining, and mitigation of personal and corporate poverty had set in. In addition, the missions had suffered a blow in 1291, when the Saracens took Acre, the last Christian foothold in Palestine.

The Masters General

The first two masters of the fourteenth century had short terms of office. Albert Chiavari lived only three months after his election in 1300. Bernard of Jusix, elected in 1301, died two years later. During this period, Pope Boniface VIII issued the bull, *Super cathedram,* which regulated the conflict between the friars and the diocesan clergy. Its stipulation that the mendicant Orders should pay to the diocesan clergy a fourth of the income derived from their ministry, including legacies, worked great hardships and placed the strict poverty of the Order in danger. Though the successor of Boniface, the Dominican Benedict XI, repealed the bull, Clement V reissued it.

Two masters general governed the Order between 1304 and 1317. Elected in 1304, Aylmer of Piacenza resigned in 1311 because, it was rumored, he was not sympathetic to the suppression of the Knights Templar. Berengar of Landorra governed from 1312 to 1317. He was followed by Hervey of Nedellec, an outstanding theologian (1318-1323), Barnabas Cagnoli of Vercelli (1324-1332), and Hugh of Vaucemain (1333-1341). Hugh came into conflict with Benedict XII, who was planning to reform the Order as he had the Cistercians, Franciscans and Canons Regular. The pope began by calling the master general and about twenty prominent friars to Avignon to consult with them about the subject. For this reason he cancelled the general chapter, scheduled to meet in 1338. Benedict ran into the stone-wall resistance of the general, who withstood his plans until death. Contemporary sources are vague in reporting the reasons for his opposition, and no agreement exists among modern historians. Hugh did not object to the elimination of abuses; actually, he and chapters he convened enacted many ordinances to stop them. The conflict went much deeper. Contemporaries indicate that Benedict contemplated making fundamental changes in the Dominican Constitutions. Mortier and Mandonnet suggest that Benedict wanted the Order to change from its strict poverty without ownership to dependence on property-holding and fixed income, but this does not seem to have been the case. Not choosing to impose his ideas, Benedict sought to gain his objectives through the voluntary cooperation of the master and the leading men of the Order. Their refusal to accept his plans caused the clash. With the deaths of the two antagonists (Hugh of Vaucemain died in 1341; Benedict in 1342), the danger of an essential modification in the Constitutions had passed.

Hugh of Vaucemain began a series of French masters general who governed the Order until 1379, a year after the outbreak of the Western Schism. Hugh's four immediate successors had short terms, owing to death or promotion. Gerard of Domaro de la Garde, elected on May 18, 1342, had governed but four months when Clement VI, his relative, appointed him cardinal on September 20. He enjoyed his new dignity not much longer than he had the generalate, dying fifty-three weeks after his appointment. Pierre of Baume-les-Dames held office from his election in 1343 until his death in 1345. His successor, Garin de Gy-l'évêque (1346), fell victim to the plague in August, 1348. John of Moulins, elected the following Spring, became a cardinal in December, 1350. Such brief terms were unfortunate in a time when leadership was needed to check the worsening state of religious spirit and discipline. The intervals between generals and the shortness of their tenures impeded effective leadership and accentuated the drift toward decline.

Then followed two longer generalates. During his fourteen years of leadership, Simon of Langres (1352-1366) made a determined attempt to deal with the major problems and the havoc wrought in the Order, as in the Church itself, by the Black Death. This sternness apparently earned Simon the dubious distinction of being the only general turned out of office by the Order itself—invalidly. His inability to give full attention to the Order, owing to the frequent diplomatic missions the pope entrusted to him, probably added to the murmuring against him. The general chapter of 1360 removed him from office by the narrow vote of eight to six. The minority diffinitors, joined by other friends, appealed to Innocent VI who invalidated the action. Six years later, Urban V terminated Simon's services to the Order by appointing him Bishop of Nantes. His ability and the eighteen years he lived after his elevation—he was master in theology, an able diplomat, and had been provincial of France —indicate the loss the Order sustained when he was made a bishop.

Fortunately Simon's place was taken by Elias Raymond, who also had a lengthy term. Elected in 1367, he governed the entire Order until the Western Schism divided it. As a Frenchman, Simon followed his country in 1379 in giving allegiance to Clement VII, the antipope who had taken up residence at Avignon. Elias continued as general until his death in 1389 in the Avignon Obedience of the Order.

The provinces that remained faithful to Urban VI, the first of the Roman line of papal claimants, elected Raymond of Capua, spiritual director and disciple of Catherine of Siena, in 1380. He lived until 1399. Meanwhile three masters general governed in the Avignon Obedience—Nicholas of Troia, a Neopolitan, Nicholas of Valladolid, a Spaniard, and John of Puinoix, a Frenchman, natives of the areas and provinces that followed Avignon. The last of the three held office from 1399 to the end of the Schism in 1418. Then he resigned and the Council of Constance rewarded him with an episcopate.

The Order did not escape the doubt and confusion that settled over Christendom when the Western Schism began. Since it was almost impossible for any but those closest to events to judge correctly the claims of the papal rivals, nations settled their allegiance to one or other claimant on the basis of national interest. Divided countries or border regions saw rival claimants to bishoprics and abbeys. Orders that were united under a central government, like the Dominicans, followed a similar pattern. The French, Spanish, and Neopolitan provinces, and the friars of Scotland gave allegiance to Avignon; the others adhered to Rome. After 1380 the Order had a double series of general chapters and masters general. The province of Germany, located in a politically divided country, had two provincials, but the larger number of priories followed Peter Eglin, who was loyal to Rome. The universal doubt is symbolized by the Dominican saints of the time. Closer to the facts, Catherine of Siena and

Raymond of Capua served Urban VI of Rome. Vincent Ferrer used all his eloquence and learning to persuade the clergy, kings, and peoples of the Spanish Peninsula to unite behind Clement VII, the Avignon claimant.

The Chapters

The Order changed its Constitutions in 1374 to permit the summoning of general chapters every two or three years instead of annually, a move undoubtedly influenced by the unsettled conditions of the age—the papal conflicts, the Hundred Years War, the Black Plague, and the Schism. The new measure also worked a subtle change in Dominican government, increasing the power and influence of the general and decreasing that of the chapters. In line with the growing power of kings in the political field, this change may reflect a lessening of confidence in representative procedures within the Order. The following table illustrates the declining influence of the chapters.

Number of General Chapters 306

13th century	75	
14th century	76	18 chapters were held during the 14-15
15th century	47	centuries in the Avignon Obedience
16th century	28	
17th century	20	
18th century	6	
19th century	11	
20th century	24	(including the 1974 chapter)

Though the general chapter has met less frequently since 1370, it continues to be a powerful bond of unity. It supplies the master general with advice, counsel, and information about the Order, implements his programs, acquaints the leading friars of the Order with one another, provides concerted action, and makes new laws. Dominican history seems to show that the general chapter acts as a barometer. When it meets regularly and does its work thoroughly, the Order's discipline and ministry seem to flourish. Infrequent meetings appear to accompany periods of stagnation.

When the chapters became less frequent, more of the Order's business fell into the hands of the master. Though we have no means of comparison, since the letters of Raymond of Capua are the first to survive, a look at his *Register* shows the multiplicity of cases that reached his desk. Many of his decisions, it would seem, should have been handled at the local level of government. Probably the troubled times of Schism and the low state of discipline partly account for this recourse to higher authority.

Though the general's position was strengthened by the infrequency of chapters, he found his authority curbed by the appointment of a cardinal protector, a new feature in Dominican life. The Order's strong government was exercised with so much corporate responsibility that, contrary to the practice of the Holy See with regard to other Orders, it did not appoint a protector for it until 1373, when Gregory XI named Cardinal William of Aigrefeuille. The protector's duties were never clearly defined, but expanded as time went on. During the next two centuries, they widened to such an extent that the cardinal began to deal with the internal affairs of the Order in the same manner as the master. The conflict between reformed and unreformed friars during the fifteenth century, and the trend toward centralization that developed in the Church itself during the sixteenth, account for this growth. Since 1887, when Leo XIII assumed personal protection of the Order, recent popes have acted in this capacity.

The Provinces

When the provinces were first divided between 1294 and 1303, their number climbed to eighteen. Seventy-five years later the fission process began again. The chapter of 1378 made the island of Sicily a province and took the first step toward making Dalmatia one. Urban VI declared it a province later that year when the Schism began. The new provinces were smaller than their predecessors, permitting greater cohesion among the friars and closer contact between them and the provincials.

The Preaching Ministry

Despite the lower level of its religious life, the Order continued to develop noteworthy preachers. In the first half of the century, James Passavanti exercised a fruitful preaching ministry in the Church of Santa Maria Novella in Florence, where he was one of the leading friars for many years. He was also a spiritual writer whose works influenced the developing Italian vernacular. He composed his *Mirror of True Penance* from the elements of a lenten course preached in 1354. The work strongly reflects the troubled times that followed on the plague. It emphasizes the fear of God, though Passavanti also mentions the joy that comes from a penitential life.

At the peak of a successful preaching career in 1335, Venturino of Bergamo sought to bring peace to the troubled cities of northern Italy through preaching and by leading a pilgrimage to the Eternal City. The progress of the pilgrims through Italy was marked by great enthusiasm and signs of penance wherever they passed. After the pilgrimage had been in Rome for some days and the problem of feeding and housing many thousands of pilgrims became acute, Venturino panicked in a moment of weakness and fled secretly. The irrepressible friar quickly regained his composure and traveled to Avignon, hoping to interest Benedict XII in a crusade. Instead, the irate pontiff scolded him for coming unannounced into the papal apartments, penanced him for imprudent remarks made during the pilgrimage, and for the disturbances it caused in Rome. Then he banished him to a remote priory. Clement VI, the next pope, rehabilitated him in 1343 and sent him off to preach a crusade in Lombardy. After a year of preaching, Venturino joined the crusading army and accompanied it to Smyrna. There he died in 1346 after an exhausting month preaching, encouraging the besieged crusaders, and nursing the sick.

Venturino also ranks as a writer of spiritual letters and treatises. He corresponded with the German Dominican mystics, and was friendly with John Tauler, also a great preacher. Venturino, Meister Eckhart, Henry Suso, and Tauler worked closely with nuns, preaching to them and guiding them. This was also true of John Dominici, an outstanding preacher toward the end of the century. Venice, Pisa, and Florence enjoyed his powerful lenten courses. He established the monastery of Corpus Christi in Venice and sent the nuns numerous letters dealing with the spiritual life.

The preachers of the Order also continued to publish sermon collections and other homiletic writings. Thomas of Wales produced an important book on the method of preaching. John Bromyard, another English Dominican, completed a homiletic encyclopedia, the *Summa praedicantium,* just before 1350. A vast alphabetical collection of theological lore and sermon materials, it was a valuable source book for preachers. Historians now find it important for studying the preaching and culture of the century.

In the late fourteenth century Archbishop Fitzralph of Dublin renewed the attacks the diocesan clergy had made on the ministry of the friars a century before. He carried his complaints to the papal court, but though he was an able orator and writer, Fitzralph was unable to gain any alteration in the basic relationship between the religious and diocesan clergy.

Studies and Theology

As the Order entered its second century, it could be proud of its academic record and the eminence of its theologians. It had appreciated Thomas Aquinas and valued his doctrine during his lifetime and defended both after his death. During the opening years of the fourteenth century the Order took a more determined stand in favor of his doctrine. The impetus was provided by Durandus of Saint Pourçain, one of its most talented members, during the academic year of 1307-1308. As a bachelor of the *Sentences* at Paris, he developed opinions notably different from Thomas. Obviously reacting to Durandus, the 1309 chapter required lectors and sublectors to teach according to the doctrine of Thomas and students to study his works diligently. Those who failed to comply were "to be punished gravely and quickly." In 1312 Durandus took his licentiate; Clement V appointed him to teach at the papal university before Lent, 1313. The chapter of that year then spoke even more decidedly in favor of Thomism, commanding that no brother dare in his teaching "to assert anything contrary to what is commonly believed to be the opinion" of Thomas; lectors were ordered to expound some of his articles. The chapter required provincials to watch over the work of lectors and remove those who violated its commands. It revived a thirteenth-century measure calling for the censorship of books. The next chapter entrusted the immediate supervision of lectors and students to the student master.

The Order was not only concerned with Thomism when it took these steps. It felt that the opinions of Durandus endangered the teaching of the Church. The 1313 ordinance stipulated that lectors were not to "dare to assert anything contrary to the common judgment of the doctors" in matters pertaining to faith or morals, except to refute it. Under attack Durandus did modify some of his extreme views.

A number of able scholars, who ranked with the disciples of Thomas in their solidity and depth of doctrine and loyalty to their master, matched the learning of Durandus. The foremost was Hervey of Nedellec, who became master general in 1318, and waged a theological war with Durandus that lasted for almost two decades. The others were John of Naples, Peter de la Palu, John of Lausanne, James of Viterbo, William Peter Godin, and Armand of Belvezer. Almost all of them were drawn into the literary controversy with Durandus.

The Order also took steps to keep its studies at the peak of efficiency. The 1305 chapter devoted attention to the Order's academic organization, issuing directions for the houses of studies. The chapters of 1313 to 1315 promulgated detailed instructions for students and professors. They adjusted the number of students to be sent to each house and regulated the appointment and teaching of professors. To ensure efficient academic performance, they set up norms for attendance at lectures, protected the rights and privileges of students, curbed any extraneous activities on their part, and provided for their books and clothing. They called on priories to stock or establish their libraries.

The Durandus affair was not the only theological concern of

Dominicans during these years. Master General Barnabas Cagnoli of Vercelli and other theologians took a determined stand against an erroneous opinion that Pope John XXII held as a private theologian. John maintained that those who died in grace would not enjoy the Beatific Vision until judgment day. The courageous opposition of Thomas of Wales, who preached against the opinion at Avignon, John's residence, cost him many years in the papal prison.

Controversy with the disciples of Duns Scotus also began at this time. Scotus was a Franciscan contemporary of Durandus who also worked out an original system of theology. His most notable contribution was to lay down the principle which enabled theologians to develop the doctrine of the Immaculate Conception. With few exceptions, Dominican theologians challenged this and other points in the teaching of Scotus. They kept up resistance to the Immaculate Conception for centuries because they thought Thomas had opposed it, waging a losing battle against its increasing acceptance by theologians and the faithful. Even the Spanish Dominican provinces endorsed it. Nevertheless, the Dominican stand was very important for the development of the doctrine and illustrates how doctrines are clarified. They forced its defenders to re-examine their position constantly. The last serious problems raised by the Immaculate Conception were not adequately solved for several centuries and were not completely removed until its definition in 1854.

The posture adopted by the Order and its theologians during the Durandus, Beatific Vision, and Immaculate Conception controversies indicate that its awareness of its doctrinal mission in the Church had already evolved.

Despite this doctrinal activity, the Order's intellectual life began to suffer as scholasticism declined and religious discipline decayed. Dominican schools and scholars were hurt by the Black Death. Later in the century, academic efforts were again hampered by the Western Schism. Perhaps these facts explain the failure of Thomists, who had reacted vigorously to Durandus and other opponents, to recognize the dangers inherent in Nominalism, a new school of thought headed by William of Ocham. The Church itself pronounced no formal condemnation. By the end of the century, Nominalism had made the University of Paris its chief stronghold and, in the fifteenth century, gained a strong position at German universities. Thomas Holcot, an English Dominican, did not escape its influence, and Thomas Crathorn, another member of the English province, completely accepted it. The first Thomistic challenge to Nominalism came from John Capreolus early in the next century.

The German Dominican Mystics

During the fourteenth century, as in other periods of trouble and trial, men looked to the spiritual leaders for hope and guidance. The divisions, strife, and war that accompanied the lengthy controversy between the popes and the Emperor turned the minds of good people toward prayer and penance as the answer to the vexing problems of the time. Mysticism flowered up and down the Rhine Valley. Jan van Ruysbroeck led the movement in the Netherlands, the Dominicans in Germany.

The Order's own contemplative apostolic life, aiming at intimate union with God, bears within itself the seeds of mysticism. Historically, the Dominican preaching and teaching ministry forged links between the friars and people who thirsted for a life of union with God—priests, nuns, laymen, and beguines (celibate women who lived a spiritual life without vows, either singly or in community). Dominic and Jordan of Saxony established the ties that existed between Dominican friars and nuns. Henry of Cologne, Siger of Lille, and Walter of Strassburg worked among devout women in Ghent, Lille, and Germany. St. Juliana of Liege derived support largely from Dominicans when she struggled to introduce the feast of Corpus Christi. Henry of Halle and other friars were closely associated with St. Gertrude and the two Saint Mechtildas at the Cistercian monastery of Helfta, within whose walls devotion to the Sacred Heart flourished.

The German mystics of the fourteenth century were the heirs of this tradition of cooperation with religious people. Though others were drawn within the radius of the German mystical movement, Dominicans were predominant. It traces its origins to Albert the Great and his disciples. Meister Eckhart (d. 1327), was its theoretician, John Tauler (d. 1361) its preacher, and Henry Suso (d. 1366) its poet. A wide circle of religious and lay people, called Friends of God, who worked and prayed for spiritual renewal, gathered around these leaders. The mysticism of the school is called speculative, because it sought to probe and record the depths of man's sanctification and union with God. This is especially true of the writings of Eckhart. His writings and those of Tauler and Suso are the monuments of German mysticism. Suso's *Little Book of Eternal Wisdom,* one of the best-loved works of the Middle Ages, is a perennial classic. A remarkable series of biographies and chronicles, written in seven of the monasteries, bears witness to the intense mystical life that flowered among the Dominican nuns during this time.

In 1329, about a year after Meister Eckhart's death, John XXII condemned as heretical seventeen propositions extracted from his writings and eleven others as rash and suspect of heresy. Convinced of his good intentions and innocence, Eckhart spent too much time during his defense emphasizing his orthodoxy and failed to challenge the propositions. This poorly conceived defense, together with the unscientific method of judging propositions outside their context, explains why theologians could place under a cloud the teaching and memory of a theologian who was never a willing heretic.

Dealing with profound and difficult concepts, often in the vernacular, Eckhart tried to convey the fruits of his own deep experiences and reflection. Using a vigorous style in tune with the spirit of the German language, he produced a prose that was unmatched at the time and exercised a lasting influence on the German tongue. As a developing language, it was inadequate for conveying the profound ideas about God and the soul that are difficult to express in any language. Eckhart often coined words or adapted Latin idioms to serve his purpose and occasionally used paradox and hyperbole. In addition, his hearers sometimes took down his words inaccurately. At times he himself was not sufficiently precise. It is not surprising then that some of his comments lend themselves to a pantheistic or a quietistic interpretation. A discerning reader or one using a text accompanied by explanatory notes, might read his works with profit.

The German Dominicans did not have a monopoly on spiritual writings or mysticism. A number of authors also flourished in Italy. James Passavanti and Venturino of Bergamo have already appeared in another part of this chapter. Catherine of Siena, a member of the Third Order, was the greatest of them all. As far as can be judged here below, she surpassed the German mystics in personal holiness and outstripped her own countrymen in the excellence of her writing—the *Dialogue of Divine Providence*, her prayers, and her letters. They are all rich in doctrine.

A true Dominican, Catherine undertook works of mercy, especially the care of the sick, guided an ever-growing family of disciples, and sought to bring peace to the warring families of the Tuscan countryside. Deeply concerned for the welfare and reform of the Church, she worked for the reconciliation of Florence and Gregory XI, contributed to the definitive return of the popes from Avignon to Rome, and did all she could to heal the Western Schism, which broke out two years before her death. In her anguish over the suffering Church, she offered herself as a victim for it. Surrounded by disciples, she died in Rome on April 29, 1380. The *Life of Catherine*, written by Raymond of Capua, her confessor, and various minor pieces, record her apostolic works and mystical experiences. Pius II, a fellow Sienese, canonized her. Pius XII named her and Francis of Assisi the chief patron saints of Italy, and Paul VI declared her a Doctor of the Church.

The Decline of Spirit and Discipline

Late in its first century, the Order entered a decline-decay crisis that reached a climax in widespread collapse of spirit and religious discipline. The crisis originated in the multiplicity of problems that characterized the times and plagued the Church and all the Orders. Besides, at the middle of the century (1342-1352) four masters general had such short terms of office that the Order lacked firm leadership at a critical time. The Order's own ideals now began to work against it. Its strict discipline, poverty and the incessant study required for the preaching ministry demand a constant renewal of zeal. What the early generations of friars had been able to do because of their dedication and spirit, their brothers of the fourteenth century failed to achieve. The tensions inherent in the contemplative apostolic life became destructive when they were not solved by men of strong motivation and zeal.

The signs of decline began to appear about 1290. They became notably worse about 1325 and reached their peak after the Black Death, 1348-1349. The general confusion that descended on the Church thirty years later, when the Western Schism began, made it more difficult to deal with these problems. The Order made a valiant attempt to solve them. The encyclicals of the masters general and the ordinances and admonitions of general chapters lashed out at prevailing abuses. The number of ordinances and admonitions increase in scope and number after 1325. By mid-century they have become very long, covering complete pages of printed text, regulating points of religious life, study, and ministry.

The progress in decline can be seen by comparing the encyclicals of Munio of Zamora with those of Hervey Nedellec. In his 1285 encyclical Munio demanded a more serious practice of poverty, more attention to silence, and greater love of the cell. In another letter he spoke against idleness and required greater devotion to study. Forty years later (1323), while extolling the virtues of the common life—love, peace, humility, voluntary poverty, and purity of life—and calling for dedication to study and the preaching ministry, Hervey of Nedellec demanded that superiors punish the unruly and insolent who were not living up to their obligations. He himself intended to deal with friars who presumed to throw off the religious yoke and, with the aid of outsiders, ambitiously sought to improve their position. Hervey's tone and the points he deals with indicate a change for the worse since the days of Munio.

The accelerating decline that was evident when Hervey wrote turned to decay twenty-five years later after the bubonic plague had done its work. Statistics speak louder than words. In Florence, 80 Dominicans died, in Pisa, 40, in Lucca, 20, in Basel, 11. The Florentine monastery of St. James at Ripoli lost 100 nuns. The province of Provence lost 378 members. After burying all the Franciscans of Carcassonne and his own brethren, William of Garric also sank into the grave. Imitating townspeople who tried to avoid infection by fleeing to the countryside, frightened friars deserted their infected priories. The epidemic recurred, especially in 1401 when the Avignon Obedience lost 1,100 Dominicans.

The Black Death left behind it empty priories and devastated provinces. Herculean efforts and wise policies were needed for the rebuilding of community life. All the Orders made two important mistakes. They tried to man all their empty priories, spreading their personnel too thin, and they recruited young and poorly educated boys who were so immature that they had to be given wholesale dispensations from religious discipline. When they grew older, these boy-religious were so accustomed to a soft life that no one could call them to anything stricter.

The difficulty of implementing the poverty of the Order, which forbade holding possessions and fixed revenues, was one of the chief causes of decline. Suited to a small band of dedicated, mature, and trained preachers, strict poverty posed great problems as soon as the Order's membership climbed into the thousands. In the fourteenth century, priories began to hold properties, rents, annuities, and fixed incomes. They acquired mills, granges, houses, and endowments. The practice began innocently enough in the thirteenth century, when the generosity of the faithful could no longer keep pace with the Order's growing numbers and expanding curriculum of studies. Larger buildings, more books, and increased income were needed to care for larger numbers of young untrained men. In some places the friars gave silent witness to their declining spirit when they built large and costly churches, cloisters, and buildings with the help of rich benefactors.

The acquisition of properties in the cities caused external difficulties as well. Municipal governments and townspeople often resented the loss of property that could be taxed and inherited.

They imposed sanctions on the friars; in some places boycotted and blocked their priories. Strassburg and Cologne exiled the community until a compromise was reached. Political conflicts also made the practice of poverty burdensome. When Dominicans remained loyal to the pope and preached the ecclesiastical penalties against Louis of Bavaria, cities loyal to the Emperor forbade their citizens to give alms to the friars or exiled them, as at Constance and Strassburg, the communities of Suso and Tauler.

As the Order found it increasingly difficult to care for them, friars developed independent resources. They appealed to their families and friends for books, habits, and necessities. Abuse set in when friars sought comfort and security by acquiring legacies, gifts, and annuities. Vanity in clothing appeared; habits were made of better cloth, or ampler cut, and were often decorated with rows of buttons, wide cuffs, pleats, and sometimes trains. Friars with incomes preempted space in the dormitories, turned cells into rooms, or built apartments with private entrances through which servants, friends, and women could enter. Cells were lavishly decorated and became the place for frivolous and lengthy recreations. Talented friars vied to become preachers general and to graduate as masters for the sake of the honor, privileges, and perquisites. Softness of life, accompanied by laxity of discipline and neglect of learning, entered Dominican priories. After 1350 the choir, refectory, and classrooms were deserted as often as they were frequented. Only poor friars who could not provide well for themselves came to the refectory. When the bottom was reached, tradesmen wheeled their carts into the refectory and peddled their wares to friars who could pay for them. Fast and abstinence became a memory and dispensations the rule. Community life had broken down and the private life had replaced it. This was the state of affairs in many of the houses of the Order soon after 1350, but the entering wedges had been driven earlier.

John Bromyard's preaching encyclopedia puts words in the mouth of a lazy friar that show how the declining spirit of the Order was hampering the ministry: "I wish to live peacefully in the cloister, reading and chanting. I do not care to hasten about the world, since this brings with it much fatigue, the great responsibility of hearing confessions and of the apostolic ministry, and the shame and labor of begging for alms." Writing about the worst state of affairs, and perhaps exaggerating for effect, John Dominici, the leader of reform in Italy, raised the veil on the abuses and pointed to their remedy: "Let them first refrain from unnecessary buildings, reintroduce the common life, give up social superfluities, spend no money at the papal court in their private interest, and then, after the example of Dominic, let them go two by two to preach and collect alms."

First Attempts at Reform

Tuscan friars made the first attempt to bolster discipline shortly after 1300. Nicknamed "spirituals," because they bore some resemblance to a Franciscan group that advocated strict adherence to the letter of the Rule and Testament of Francis, they received attention at the general chapter of 1312 and the provincial chapters of the Roman province then and subsequently. Though they did not emphasize poverty excessively, they apparently drifted into unacceptable positions which destroyed their movement. An official attempt at reform began in 1369, promoted by Stephen Lacombe, provincial of the Roman province and vicar of the master general in Italy. His adherence to the Avignon Obedience in 1378 nullified his efforts.

The influence of Catherine of Siena and her disciples led to the first permanent and successful reform movement. Their opportunity came when Raymond of Capua became master general in the Roman Obedience in 1380. During his tours of visitation Raymond found friars everywhere who were truly given to the service of God and wished to serve Him in regular discipline according to the Constitutions. In Germany, Conrad of Prussia had achieved an informal leadership over these men. When Raymond came on visitation in 1388, he gave Conrad the priory of Colmar to begin a reform there.

Raymond's next step was to universalize what he had done in Germany. With the approval of the 1388 general chapter, he sent out an encyclical calling on all the provinces to found a priory of strict observance and mendicant poverty. Once friars were formed in these houses, Raymond intended to send them to other priories, hoping in this way to reform the whole Order. The next June he appointed Conrad of Prussia vicar general over Colmar and two monasteries of nuns. By that time Conrad had thirty friars under his jurisdiction and the reform was well launched. It reached a conclusion in the German province in 1475 when most of the friars had accepted reform and were strong enough to control the provincial chapter and elect the provincial. It was the first province to reform itself. A handful of its unreformed priories were placed under a vicar general of their own. John Dominici began the reform in Italy. He introduced observance into the priories at Venice, Chioggia, and Città di Castello. He founded the Venetian monastery of Corpus Christi and encouraged Clara of Gambacorta and Maria Mancini in the monastery of Pisa.

The reformed priories and their vicars remained under the control of their provinces, but in many matters Raymond exempted them from the provincial's authority and reserved decisions to himself. These steps led later to the grouping of reformed priories into congregations, a feature of the reform not in Raymond's original plans but made necessary by unreformed friars who hampered and opposed the reform movement. Despite all resistance, it continued to gain strength. Half a century after Raymond's death, John Uytenhove estimated that there were 200 reformed priories and monasteries in the province of Rome, Lombardy, Spain, Aragon, Germany, and Saxony.

Raymond's plan of reform was superior to the earlier approaches toward renewal. They had always dealt with disciplinary problems by means of penances and legislation, multiplying them as decline accelerated. The friars could not have taken very seriously the multiplicity of prohibitions, threats, and penalties that clutter the acts of the general chapters. If they had, these would not have been repeated and increased year after year. Hugh of Vaucemain, early in the century, and John of Moulins at its middle, were groping toward Raymond's plan. Hugh planned to provide better training for novices by gathering them into novitiate houses; John sought to make Paris both a training center of studies and religious observance. Returning to their priories on the completion of their training, friars so prepared could become a good leaven. Neither proposal was carried through. Excellent in themselves, they placed too much burden on the young alone and could not have succeeded against the kind of opposition the reformers later endured. Raymond's plan was also utopian to some degree. Premised on the cooperation of all, it did not work as smoothly or well as he had hoped. But with true insight he had grasped that renewal and reform cannot be legislated but come about only when persons are strongly motivated to live voluntarily according to the Rule and Constitutions. He sought to reaffirm the religious life and reestablish the contemplative base of the Order's ministry.

The Order's fourteenth century was a very human one, reflecting both worthwhile achievement and shocking weaknesses. The zeal, sometimes sanctity, of men who sought to check decline and renew Dominican life compensated for the defects. The prayer of the mystics, the writings of scholars, the collected sermons of preachers, and the initiation of reform point to the strength inherent in the Order's timeless mission and lofty ideal. The rise of the German mystics, the holiness of women like Catherine of Siena, Clara Gambacorta, Maria Mancini, and the nuns of the German monasteries, and of men like Henry Suso, Raymond of Capua, and John Dominici highlight the Order's vitality and the reservoir of spiritual strength it could draw upon even during a time of confusion and decline.

CHAPTER V

FIFTEENTH CENTURY—THE LIFE AND MINISTRY OF THE ORDER

The fifteenth century opened with much hope for the Order. A firm reform was under way, and the Western Schism was moving toward a close. As long as it lasted the Order was handicapped by division, but this wound was soon healed.

The Schism, the appointment of a cardinal protector, and triennial general chapters contributed to the development of the master general's powers and curia, and his residence at Rome. Originating earlier, these changes reached maturity during the fifteenth century. It was already the custom for the master general, when not on tours of visitation, to live wherever the pope resided. Adhering to the Roman claimant, Raymond of Capua took up residence at Santa Maria sopra Minerva at the beginning of the Schism. The priory became the permanent home of the master. The register of Raymond, in which his secretary recorded digests, and sometimes complete texts, of letters he wrote, is the first letter-book of any master to survive. Then there is a gap until the last quarter of the fifteenth century. From then on the series of registers is almost complete, an indication that the establishment of a fixed residence for the general led to the development of archives and a staff of assistants. From the earliest days he had had the help of a consultant, secretary, and a cooperator brother. The procurator general, who had charge of business with the Holy See, joined the group when residence was established in Rome.

A minor innovation occurred early in the century when the Order began using a coat-of-arms. It was the "Mantle Shield," featuring the parted black mantel of the habit on a white field.

Often the dog of St. Dominic was placed below the mantel. From the end of the century, when the coat was printed on the title page of books, the Order used it until the "Lily Shield" replaced it in the twentieth century. The assumption of a coat-of arms, a device used by military men and the aristocracy, manifests the growing self-awareness of the Order and, perhaps, a growing pretension as well.

The Masters General

The twelve masters of the fifteenth century were able men, though three of them had such short terms that we can judge only by their earlier life. Peter Rochin was general for twenty-five days in 1450, Guy Flamochet twenty-six months in 1451, and Barnabas Sansoni one month in 1486. The terms of Thomas Paccaroni (1401-1414), Leonard Dati (1414-1425), and Bartholomew Texier (1426-1449), span almost fifty years. Six other masters also served; Martial Auribelli, twice.

Though the Council of Pisa attempted to solve the Schism in 1409, it made matters worse by electing a third claimant, Alexander V. However, his election did cause a realignment in the Order. John Puinoix, master general of the Avignon Obedience, found himself governing only the friars of Spain, Aragon, and Scotland, countries still faithful to Avignon. In the Roman Obedience, which now embraced only parts of Germany and Italy and the Kingdom of Naples, Gregory XII appointed a vicar general for the Dominicans loyal to him. Since most of the provinces united behind Paccaroni, who had been master in the Roman Obedience before the Council of Pisa and was now master in the Obedience of Pisa, the task of healing the wounds the Schism had inflicted on the Order could begin.

Leonard Dati was elected general in 1414, the year the Council of Constance began. It was his task to reunite the Order when the Council solved the Schism in 1417, electing Martin V, a pope universally recognized. John Puinoix, Dati's counterpart in the Avignon Obedience, resigned his office and was promoted to the bishopric.

Bartholomew Texier, elected in 1426 by the unusual procedure of compromise, governed longer than any other master before him. During his twenty-three years in office, the Order recovered much of its earlier vitality. Its theologians took outstanding parts at the Councils of Basel and Ferrara-Florence, and more than 100 Dominicans were elevated to episcopal rank. Encouraged by Texier, the reform of the Order gained momentum and solidarity.

Martial Auribelli (1453-1462) immortalized himself when he composed the office of Vincent Ferrer, canonized in 1455 by Calixtus III. He signified his authorship by an acrostic formed by the first letter of the opening word of each stanza of the hymn for first vespers. It reads *Marialis Auribelli fecit*—"Martial Auribelli composed this." He was the only general who had two terms, serving for a total of seventeen years. To reach this distinction he had to live through the unpleasant experience of being removed from office by Pius II in 1462. The reasons that motivated Pius are nowhere to be found, but Auribelli's first encyclical after he returned to office in 1465, after Pius was in the grave, strongly hints at injustice. Strained relations between Auribelli and the reformed Congregation of Lombardy seem to have been an important factor. It was more disagreement than injustice. Auribelli defended his rights vigorously, whereas the Congregation was moving toward semi-independence, gaining all it wanted from Pius II in 1459. Auribelli was not an enthusiastic reformer but he supported reform and had granted important privileges to the Lombards.

Conrad of Asti, his successor (1462-1465), was a former vicar general of the Congregation. He suffered the same fate as Auribelli, giving up the generalate three years after election to permit his predecessor to resume the post a second time (1465-1473). When Auribelli was rehabilitated in 1465, Paul II gave the Order full liberty to manage its affairs, but then, "for just reasons," as the 1465 chapter put it, suspended Conrad from the exercise of his powers. The general could scarcely do anything but resign. The chapter unanimously reelected Auribelli. Conrad lived out his remaining years quietly, apparently never harboring any bitterness. Auribelli could not reach those heights. In his re-election encyclical he spoke bluntly, sparing neither Pius, who was not named, nor Conrad, who was.

During his second term Auribelli went through another unfortunate experience in 1468. On the heels of a conspiracy to oust him again, engineered by an Italian faction, Paul II suspended him, appointing Leonard Mansuetis vicar general, and a panel of judges to investigate the case. The cost to the Order was an invalid general chapter in 1468, nullified by the Pope when he learned that the vicar general had presided over it in contravention of the Constitutions. After a suspension of three months, Auribelli was cleared. He returned to control and rounded out five more years as general.

Leonard Mansuetis (1474-1480), former provincial of the Roman province and master of the sacred palace at the time of his election, was a learned man. He was in epistolary correspondence with Cardinal Torquemada, Marsilo Ficino, and other philosophers and humanists of the time. At his death he bequeathed his magnificent library, containing 323 manuscripts and 131 incunabula to his native priory at Perugia. Probably commissioned by the chapter that elected him, Leonard petitioned Sixtus IV to change the Order's traditional poverty to allow it to own property. The petition was granted on June 1, 1475. Some historians judge that the regime opened a new era for the Order by solving the problems that mendicant poverty had raised since the end of the thirteenth century.

The terms of the next three generals cover a short five years. Salvo Cassetta governed for two years and three months (June 10, 1481 to September 15, 1483). Bartholomew Comazio was general for less than ten months. Elected on October 10, 1484, he was stricken at Perugia while ministering to the victims of the plague and died on the feast of St. Dominic, 1485. Barnabas Sansoni held office from June 29 to July 29, 1486.

Joachim Torriani (1487-1500) closed the century. A learned man, skilled in both Greek and Latin, he had been provincial of the province of St. Dominic for many years before becoming general. Though he was not a member of any reformed group, he was noted for the simplicity of his life. He was content with the bare necessities of life and satisfied with one meal a day; austerities he continued as general. Toward the end of his career, he had the unpleasant experience of defrocking Savonarola and his companions just before their execution.

The Lessening of Liberty

During the fifteenth century the Order did not enjoy its customary liberty. First, the cardinal protector began to play a more active role. His powers reached such a stage of development under Cardinal Carafa, who functioned as protector from 1478 to 1511, that he became in effect a second master general. Three times from 1486 to 1490 Carafa actually acted as vicar general with full jurisdiction over the Order. He used his authority to further the Order's reform, a motive that justified the lessening of constitutional liberty. The unreformed were in control of the general and provincial governments and were using their power to hamper the reform. When Carafa became protector, the hostility between reformed and unreformed friars had reached such a pitch that only someone from outside could have saved the Order from harmful dissensions.

The Church's supervision of the Order manifested itself in several ways. Though there were some earlier precedents, the practice of calling elective chapters to Rome began during the second half of the century. This happened in the 1451, 1474, 1481, and 1501 elections. This was coupled with the presidency of the protector over the last three. Another channel of papal influence was the vicar general, who administered the Order during a vacancy in the generalship. By passing over the vicar who should have taken office constitutionally and naming a vicar, the pope was virtually nominating his candidate. This happened four times in the century, when Mansuetis was elected in 1474, Cassetta in 1481, Comazio in 1484, and Torriani in 1487. Appointment failed to obtain the post in 1486 for James Stubach, provincial of Germany. Instead, Sansoni was elected. The 1481 election illustrates another mode of influence. When Sixtus IV received the electors in audience, he assured them they enjoyed full liberty of election but declared how pleased he would be if they elected Cassetta. Not bothering to ballot, the voters chose him by acclamation.

A more dubious procedure was the appointment of substitute electors for absentees. The Western Schism planted this idea in the minds of some friars, since the number of voters in each obedience had become diminutive. When Raymond of Capua died, the friars petitioned Boniface IX for the privilege of supplying substitute electors for the provinces that had given allegiance to Avignon. Boniface granted the petition but revoked it when Vicar General Thomas Paccaroni pointed out the danger to unity involved in this departure from the Constitutions. The same wisdom was not displayed in 1426. In appointing Thomas de Regno vicar general during the vacancy, Martin V granted him authority to name substitute voters. A heated dispute erupted when the votes were counted and it was seen that the substitute votes had given the election to Thomas. When they were not counted, the election went to Louis of Valladolid. To restore peace both candidates withdrew. The chapter then appointed them to select a general; their choice fell on Bartholomew Texier. Substitute voters again appeared in 1484. Their appointment caused such a battle when the chapter convened at Pentecost that Sixtus IV sent the delegates home. His candidate, Bartholomew Comazio, an active reformer and vicar general by papal appointment, won the election in October. Master General Torriani obtained but did not use the right to appoint substitute diffinitors in 1491. This marked the end of an unfortunate experiment.

The Provinces

During this century some minor changes occurred in the governmental machinery of the provinces. Until 1410 the provincial chapter convened annually, but in that year the master general was empowered to permit biennial meetings for a just cause. Thirteen years later a change in the Constitutions permitted the provincial chapters themselves to decide whether they would meet every one or every two years. Another change came in 1407 when masters in sacred theology became members of the provincial chapter. Since this was a lifetime privilege and the masters were not elected delegates, their membership marked a move away from the traditional democracy of the Order.

The roster of provinces climbed to twenty-two by the addition of Portugal and Scotland. When the Schism broke out, the Portuguese Dominicans, joining their fellow countrymen, remained faithful to Urban VI, the true pontiff. The rest of the Spanish province adhered to Clement VII of Avignon. Martin V sanctioned the separation in 1418 by creating Portugal a province. Scotland became independent when the 1481 general chapter split it off from the English province and appointed its first provincial. The distance of the new province necessitated some concessions that prepared the Order to deal with the overseas provinces that would be created in the New World in the next century. In 1484 Comazio exempted Scotland from sending diffinitors to general chapters that met south of the Alps. Also the general provided that when it elected a provincial, it need not seek his confirmation. He delegated his powers in this instance to the three ranking priors of the province.

Ireland made a renewed attempt to achieve provincial status. Its first creation as a province in 1378 was nullified by Urban VI when the English provincial protested the action. The general chapter of 1484 again made Ireland a province, but the English friars succeeded in having the 1491 chapter undo the work on the plea that the Order could not grant a divorce when the pope had solemnized the marriage. Ireland had to wait until 1536 before it became a province.

The Monasteries and Third Order

During the fifteenth century, the number of Dominican monasteries rose somewhat above the 157 that stood in 1358, though we have no adequate catalogue. Six new foundations were made in Holland alone, and Italy saw the establishment of a number of large monasteries. In 1385 Clara of Gambacorta founded one in Pisa where the primitive rule was lived faithfully. John Dominici grounded Corpus Christi in Venice in 1394. Both became centers of reform. During the lifetime of Savonarola, the

Florentine monastery of St. Lucy housed 100 nuns and had to refuse applications of 200 candidates. Schönensteinbach in Alsace, established in 1397, was the center from which reform radiated to other monasteries in Germany and Holland. A vigorous life flourished in the reformed and newly founded monasteries. Imitating the *Lives of the Sisters* written in the thirteenth century monasteries, John Meyer, one of the leaders of the reform, described the lives of a score of nuns who lived holy lives in the German monasteries. St. Catherine's in St. Gall amassed a library of 250 books, while St. Catherine's in Nuremberg had more than 370, imposing collections for that day. They were mostly sermons, liturgical works, and spiritual classics. Some of the books still survive.

The fame of St. Catherine of Siena, who was canonized in 1461, contributed greatly to the spread of the Third Order. Reforming friars encouraged its growth and obtained from Innocent VII the confirmation of its Rule in 1405. Eugene IV approved it again in 1439. The earliest Third-Order communities, some of whom took vows, emerged during this century. Twenty-seven stood in the diocese of Constance alone. Important communities flourished in Neuenkirch, Freiburg im Breisgau, and Augsburg. The Third Order had progressed to such an extent in Germany by 1491 that Joachim Torriani promulgated ordinances for tertiaries living in community. The 1498 general chapter recommended that tertiary communities who wanted to live a more regular life adopt the Rule of Third Order enclosed communities. The Third-Order monastery of St. Catherine in Perugia, founded in 1490 by Bl. Columba of Rieti, reached a membership of fifty.

Dominican Studies

Dominican studies suffered as did every other part of the Order's life during the period of decline following the Black Death. Signs of a weakened interest in studies are not wanting in the acts of the chapters of the fourteenth and fifteenth centuries. However, the school system remained unimpaired. Occasionally the chapters had to urge provinces to fill their quotas at the general houses of studies, though evidence reveals the presence of foreign friars at the various general houses. Even the relatively obscure priory at Breslau sent its friars far and wide for their higher studies.

Traditionally Dominicans took their degrees at Paris, Oxford, and Cambridge, but the monopoly of these schools was lost during the fifteenth century when many new universities were founded. The first break in the monopoly resulted from the Western Schism. Finding their access to the University of Paris closed, friars of the Roman Obedience received permission to matriculate and graduate elsewhere. The University of Bologna, which had established a theology faculty in 1364, was accepted as a place where they might graduate. As more universities were founded, friars began to take degrees at Cologne, Vienna, Perugia, Erfurt, and Prague. The University of Paris and the priory of St. Jacques lost the preeminence they had enjoyed during the Order's first two centuries. The general chapter brought the Constitutions into accord with the situation, recognizing degree-taking at any university, provided the chapter had designated the candidates. The Hundred Years War had a similar influence. Finding travel to Paris difficult, Spanish and Portuguese friars received authorization from the 1426 general chapter to matriculate at Valladolid "and enjoy the same favors and privileges as if they had been at Paris." Seizing the opportunity presented by the foundation of many new universities, the Order also founded general houses of studies in the new university cities.

Another development was the founding of theological colleges with the power to confer degrees, a privilege granted to the houses of studies in Luchente, Aragon, in 1479, to St. Stephen's in Salamanca in 1489, and to St. Gregory's in Valladolid in 1501. The two latter colleges became the homes of some of the most outstanding Dominican theologians of the next two centuries.

Another opportunity to gain the mastership opened early in the fourteenth century, when the popes began to grant the Order the right to advance one friar to the mastership at each general chapter. At times a pope permitted the master general to promote additional candidates during the sessions. These degrees were fully earned by friars who had filled all the requirements and had passed an examination administered by masters appointed by the chapter. However, some friars in their ambition to become masters turned to influential friends outside the Order to obtain papal permission to lecture at Paris or to be advanced to the mastership out of turn. In the fifteenth century some friars received the degree by papal bull without fulfilling the requirements. These abuses and the need to codify the qualifications for earning the mastership, now that so many new universities were attended by the friars, led the general chapter to pass some much-needed legislation. On an appeal from the Order in 1402, Boniface IX attached ecclesiastical penalties to the rule that no friar might work for the mastership unless designated to do so by the general chapter. The 1403 chapter inserted into the Constitutions an academic code for graduate students that laid down a strict procedure to be followed and the requirements to be met by candidates. During the century the Order found it necessary to devote renewed attention to the problem and to further define the 1403 code.

These changes also marked the growing influence of masters in theology in the Order. Their number seems to have risen sharply during the last quarter of the fourteenth century. An indication of their growing influence was their 1407 incorporation into the provincial chapter as lifetime members. As the fifteenth century advanced masters more and more constituted the majority at general chapters until all but a few of the diffinitors held the degree.

The Thomistic School

The Thomistic School continued to gain strength as the eminence of Thomas became universally recognized. The founding of new universities, the progress of the Order's reform movement, the multiplication of manuscripts of the works of Thomas helped to spread Thomism. The followers of Thomas manifested their love for him by keeping his memory alive, propagating his cult, and studying and defending his thought. The invention of printing aided in the diffusion of his major works, the numerous commentaries on them, and expositions, manuals, and defenses.

John Capreolus, one of the greatest interpreters of Thomas, completed his *Defensiones theologiae Divi Thomae* in 1433, a work he had been writing since the early years of the century. It is a comprehensive defense and interpretation of Thomistic thought, especially as found in the *Summa theologiae*. He united in himself a profound and vast knowledge of the writings of Aquinas, his early disciples, and his adversaries.

Quoting liberally from the works of the opponents, he raises their objections and answers them. He presents the doctrine of his master sharply and clearly in the form of conclusions, marshalling texts from his works to expound each of them. No disciple of Thomas before Capreolus, and probably none since, has employed such a fullness of Thomistic texts in a single book. He heralded the Thomistic revival which would take place in the last quarter of the century in Germany, Spain, Italy, and Flanders.

Peter of Bergamo added his *Tabula aurea*, the classic index to the works of Thomas, to the Thomistic workshop. It retains its usefulness, despite the publication of an exhaustive computerized index in 1973. Peter also wrote one of the last concordances of Thomistic doctrine.

Though the *Sentences* of Peter Lombard continued to be the theological textbook in the schools and universities, theologians more and more came to appreciate the *Summa theologiae* of Thomas. It had always had a privileged and authoritative position among Dominicans. At the middle of the century, the Dominican Henry of Gorkum and the secular master John Tinctor began lecturing on it at the University of Cologne. They were followed by many Dominicans and secular masters at the universities of Rostock, Freiburg, Vienna, Leipzig, Louvain, and other German universities. One of the more outstanding lecturers on the *Summa* at Cologne in this period was Gerard of Elten. These professors also wrote the first commentaries on various parts of the *Summa*. Dominic of Flanders, professor of philosophy in several houses of study in Italy, wrote a philosophical summa, the *Summa divinae philosophiae*, which is said to have been the best synopsis of Thomism until Conrad Koellin and Thomas de Vio Cajetan wrote their commentaries on the *Summa theologiae*.

Dominican theologians argued against the doctrine of the Immaculate Conception at the Council of Basel. Apart from the Council Raphael of Pornasio and Gabriel of Barleto branded as heretics and schismatics those who held the belief. James Gil, the master of the sacred palace, was so convinced that it was erroneous that he urged Callixtus III to define Mary's conception in original sin. Unlike Cardinal John of Torquemada and John of Montenegro, who wrote and spoke against the Immaculate Conception with the objective reserve of the theologian, Vincent Bandelli employed bitterness and invective. He opposed the feast so vociferously when Sixtus IV introduced it that he merited a rebuke from the Pontiff.

Dominican Writers

Besides their books in philosophy, theology, and Scripture, Dominican authors contributed to other fields of literature as well. St. Antoninus, Archbishop of Florence (1446-1459), holds an honored place among the greatest moralists of the Church. His *Summa moralis* was a pioneering work in which moral theology came of age. His *Chronicles* or *Summa historialis* has been judged "the greatest and relatively the best historical work of the Middle Ages." He also wrote many minor ascetical and devotional treatises. St. Vincent Ferrer and the leaders of the reform movement, John Dominici, John Nider, and John Meyer, produced both homiletic and ascetical writings. Pursuing pastoral goals, they wrote for the average Christian who was engrossed in the problems of daily life and not for the spiritually elite. John Dominici's forty-two letters to the nuns of Corpus Christi taught a severe asceticism, resting on obedience, detachment, and the following of Christ. They rival those of Jordan of Saxony to Diana d'Andalo and merit him a place among the finest Italian prose writers.

Opposition to the teachings of John Wyclif and John Huss stimulated John Nider, John Stojkovic of Ragusa, and John

Torquemada to develop a significant ecclesiology that helped to stem Conciliarism and refute its theory that a general council is superior to the pope. At the end of the century Savonarola, noted chiefly for his apocalyptic preaching, wrote letters, sermons, devotional and ascetical works, scriptural commentaries, and treatises in political science that won him a secure place in the literary field. His *Triumphus crucis* was an adaptation of the *Summa contra Gentiles* of Thomas and is an early Thomistic manual of apologetics.

Fifteenth-century Dominicans made some other significant contributions to the development and dissemination of knowledge. At Salamanca their teaching about the roundness of the earth had a bearing on the discoveries of Christopher Columbus. Dominican Archbishop Diego de Deza sponsored him at the court of Ferdinand and Isabella. Two German Dominicans set up the first printing establishment in the Italian peninsula.

Though not insensitive to the new currents of thought introduced by the Renaissance and Humanism, Dominican energies were absorbed by the Order's mission to promote and sustain truth. It sensed no danger in the new developments, even though, as time went on, they necessitated modification of its attitudes and procedures. This transition in European history is marked by rediscovery of ancient classical civilization, the rise of absolute monarchy, intellectual quickening, progress in the fine arts, the growth of vernacular literatures, new scientific developments, and great economic expansion, which led to the discovery of the New World and, ultimately, to religious upheaval.

The Order had no official policy regarding the Renaissance. Until the coming of Protestantism, the changes it brought about posed no problems for the Order, since it adjusted to them gradually. Individual friars took favorable or unfavorable attitudes towards the Renaissance, especially Humanism. Though the Order was not closed to the new learning, some of its members were alert to possible abuses that lay in it, especially John Dominici, Antoninus, Savonarola, and the Dominicans at Cologne. Sensing danger to Christian morality, they felt obliged to caution against indiscriminate reading of the Classics. Their primary interests lay elsewhere (they were very busy men) but their pastoral concern moved them to issue their warnings about the pagan authors. They could scarcely fail to note that the neo-pagan tendencies they were combatting were receiving strong support from humanists in letters, tracts, and even sermons.

The traditional Dominican interest in books and libraries was heightened by the Renaissance. The Italian friars built up a number of outstanding collections and constructed some remarkable library buildings, notably at San Marco in Florence.

Many friars developed a keen interest in literature. Francis Colonna is the best known Dominican humanist. His allegorical *Dream of Poliphius,* imitating the *Speculum maius* of Vincent of Beauvais, aimed to give a compendium of the knowledge of antiquity. The work holds the distinction of being the most beautiful book printed (1499) by Aldus Manutius who was, after Gutenberg, perhaps the most famous among printers. Other Dominicans shared the linguistic approach of humanists to the Scriptures, studying the original language in which the Bible was written. Peter Schwarz, a late fourteenth-century Hebraist, holds a secure place in the history of the development of Hebrew studies in Germany. Seeking to prepare his friars for preaching and the missions, Savonarola introduced the study of Hebrew, Arabic, and Chaldean at San Marco. The priory acquired a fine library of Greek manuscripts and became the meeting place of Florentine humanists. Santes Pagnini, who achieved eminence as an orientalist in the next century, began his studies there.

Preaching

During the century the Order produced numerous outstanding preachers. St. Vincent Ferrer (d. 1419), Manfred of Vercelli (d. ca. 1431), and Savonarola (d. 1498) were so-called penance preachers, a category in which the two Franciscans, Saints Bernardine of Siena and John of Capistrano, can also be placed. Natural calamities, wars, a growing deterioration of public and private morality called forth such evangelists.

In a vision Vincent Ferrer was commissioned by the Lord, who was accompanied by St. Dominic and St. Francis, "to go through the world preaching Christ." In November, 1399, he set forth from Avignon on a twenty-year preaching career that occupied him until his death in 1419 at Vannes in Brittany. His exemplary and strict life gave his preaching an authority and power that won him a ready hearing from the people, even though he was unbending in regard to truth and his moral demands were severe. Vincent proclaimed the coming of an avenging God and used all the power of his eloquence and example to bring his congregations to conversion of life. Crowds of penitents followed him from place to place during his journeys as he visited and revisited towns and cities in Spain, southern France, upper Italy, Switzerland, northern France, and the Low Countries. Manfred of Vercelli, also a preacher of penance, imitated the style and manner of Vincent. The Italian provinces produced a number of other great preachers. They have also been beatified: John Dominici, Matthew Carreri, Andrew of Peschiera, Christopher of Milan, Mark of Modena, and Stephen Bandelli. The preaching of Savonarola in Florence dominated the closing decade of the century.

Rosary preaching was a new development, begun by Alan de la Roche when he revamped the old Marian confraternity in 1470. Renaming it the Rosary Confraternity, he prescribed recitation of the Rosary and meditation on its mysteries as the chief duty of its members. Alan saw in the devotion, with its meditations on the mysteries of the life of Jesus and Mary, an instrument of the spiritual rejuvenation needed in his day. He preached it widely, establishing the confraternity in a number of towns. Jacob Sprenger organized the mother confraternity at the Cologne priory on September 8, 1475, the very day Alan died. For a while it was necessary to be enrolled there to be a member. During a four-year period thousands of names were sent to Cologne from all over Europe; the parish of St. Mauritius in Vienna alone sent a list of 32,000 names. Alan and other members of the Congregation of Holland, one of the Order's most successful reform groups, led the preaching of the Rosary. It soon spread from the Low Countries and Germany to Italy, Spain, and other parts of Europe. The Order accepted responsibility for the Confraternity from its inception. The masters general took control of it in 1478 and began to authorize preachers to establish units and to receive members. The general chapter in 1484 and Torriani in 1487 granted a share in the spiritual works of all Dominicans. Pope Pius V confirmed the Order's control and forbade anyone but the master general to erect new branches.

The Order can rightly be called the Order of the Rosary. The Confraternity and Dominican preachers turned the Rosary, until then known chiefly in monasteries and devout circles, into a devotion practiced universally in the western Church. What the *Summa theologiae* of Thomas became for theologians, the Rosary became for other men—an epitome of Catholic doctrine. It taught the faithful of every rank and strata of society how to ponder and savor the revealed mysteries until their meaning seeped into the deepest recesses of the heart. The Rosary inspired preachers and artists. Each unit of the Confraternity was obliged to have its Rosary altar and a picture showing the fifteen mysteries. The original Rosary picture, erected at the Cologne altar, is preserved in the Church of St. Andrew, which also houses the relics of Albert the Great.

Ecclesiastical Ministries

More than a score of Friars Preachers were concerned with the solution of the great problems which exercised the Church and the Councils during the fifteenth century.

Two Dominican masters general (Leonard Dati and John Puinoix of the Avignon Obedience), and Dominican bishops and theologians helped to advance the three major concerns of the Council of Constance (1414-18): the reform of the Church, the heretical doctrines of John Wyclif and John Huss, and the solution of the Schism. When immediate preparations for the Council of Constance began, Vincent Ferrer withdrew his support from Benedict XIII, the Avignon claimant, and was instrumental in inducing the kings of the Spanish Peninsula to do likewise. John XXIII, Pisan successor to Alexander V, resigned. John Dominici worked closely with Gregory XII, the Roman claimant, was his chief advisor, and carried his resignation to the Council. The way was thus smoothed for the election of a new pope.

Martin V sent Dati as papal legate to the abortive Council of Pavia, convoked in 1423 in accord with a decree of the Council of Constance. Martin moved the assembly to Siena and brought it to an end because it was so poorly attended and inclined to enact radical decrees.

Master General Bartholomew Texier, the master of the sacred palace, the procurator general, the Order's bishops and theologians, and some provincials attended the Council of Basel. They were able to defend the privileges of the mendicant Orders when some of the Council members challenged them. The Council entrusted John of Ragusa and John Nider with important tasks during the negotiations that succeeded in bringing the Bohemian Hussites to the Council. Ragusa and Henry Kalteisen were among the four theologians chosen to respond to the Hussite articles. When Ragusa spun out his arguments for eight days, John Rokizane, the Hussite debater, quipped: "You are indeed of the Order of Preachers, that is why you talk so much." Torquemada contributed his judgment and opinion on almost every question that was agitated at the Council. He and John of Montenegro, provincial of Lombardy, were particularly prominent in defending papal rights. The Basel priory offered its hospitality to many of the conciliar sessions.

The reunion of the Greek and Latin Churches, one of the main concerns of Basel, caused a rupture between the Council and Eugene IV, when he transferred it to Ferrara to accomodate the Greeks. John of Ragusa, who was in Constantinople at the time, continued to work with Basel and became schismatic. Felix V, the antipope it elected, named him a cardinal.

The Order's contribution to the Council of Ferrara-Florence, the continuation of Basel, was so outstanding that Mortier called it the Dominican Council. More than a score of Dominican theologians were present. Andrew Chrysoberges, John of Torquemada, and John of Montenegro were among the most active participants in the debates that led to the reunion of the Churches. During the Florentine period of the Council, Eugene IV lived at the priory of Santa Maria Novella, where most of the sessions were held. After the union was effected, the pope called on several prominent friars to help implement it.

Dominican Services for the Church

The Church continued to draw Dominicans into her service during the fifteenth century as bishops, cardinals, council theologians, and ambassadors. Dominicans continued to act as inquisitors. One of them, Bartholomew of Cerverio, died at the hands of heretics in Piedmont in 1466. To handle the special difficulty created in Spain by the New Christians, converts from Judaism who did not always persevere in their new religion, Ferdinand and Isabella petitioned Sixtus IV for authority to establish the Inquisition. When it was granted they appointed two Dominicans, Michael Morillo and John of St. Martin, as inquisitors in 1480. They named Thomas Torquemada first inquisitor general in 1483. He created the supreme council and published a governing code. Diego de Deza was the only other Dominican to hold the office of grand inquisitor.

Long charged with the investigation of cases involving superstition, the medieval inquisition found its activity increased in 1484, when Innocent VIII directed Jacob Sprenger and Henry Kramer, inquisitors in Germany, to examine persons accused of witchcraft. Earlier, John Nider had written a detailed account of witchcraft in his *Ant-Book* (*Formicarius*), where he recorded the fantastic notions then current. Sprenger and Kramer published a better-known book and one that long exercised a decided influence on witchcraft trials. Their *Hammer of Witches* (*Malleus maleficarum*) dealt with the nature and evils of witchcraft and the court procedures for trying cases. Designed as a help to inquisitors, it became the textbook on sorcery and witchcraft and lay on the desk of jurists and judges, Catholic and Protestant, for a long time to come. It is still held up as a notorious symbol of the mass hysteria that spread over Catholic and Protestant Europe for several centuries.

The Missions

To complete the record of Dominican missions, we can add Vincent Ferrer's preaching to the Jews and Moslems in Spain.

Frowning on pogroms, which often broke out against Jews, he relied on preaching and persuasion as methods of conversion. Like men of his day, Vincent held that unbelievers might be compelled to come to sermons and be fined if they failed to do so. His success in making converts is probably attributable more to his sanctity than to his peaceful methods.

Art and Architecture

The Order produced an artist of first rank in Fra Angelico. His paintings at San Marco, the Vatican, and elsewhere in central Italy are universally admired and loved. James of Ulm, a cooperator brother who spent his Dominican life in Bologna, was a superb craftsman in stained-glass windows. Some Dominican priories built churches and buildings that are noteworthy as beautiful pieces of architecture—Santa Maria delle Grazie in Milan, in whose refectory Leonardo da Vinci painted his "Last Supper", Santa Maria degli Angeli in Ferrara, Santa Cruz de la Real, built for the Order at Grenada by Ferdinand and Isabella, and the plateresque-style facades of the colleges of St. Stephen at Salamanca, and St. Gregory at Valladolid. The library designed by Michelozzo for San Marco, Florence, became the model of similar buildings in Bologna, Ferrara, Perugia, and Santa Maria delle Grazie in Milan. Reflecting the gloom that ran through much of the century, the friars at Basel, Colmar, and Bern decorated their cloisters with "Dance of Death" pictures, a favorite theme in literature and art at the time.

The Order experienced both successes and failures during the fifteenth century. It was the butt of verbal attacks when Chaucer and other popular writers hurled their satire against its members, some of whom deserved it. John Wyclif made more serious charges against the friars. There was also material injury. The Hundred Years War destroyed or damaged priories and scattered the friars in France; the Hussite Wars, in Bohemia. The advancing Turks shut down many houses in Hungary. On the whole, however, the century has more on the credit than on the debit side of its Dominican ledger.

CHAPTER VI

RENEWAL AND REFORM IN THE FIFTEENTH CENTURY

The beginnings of reform reach back into the closing ten years of the fourteenth century; its history stretches through the fifteenth into the sixteenth and later centuries. Though it never succeeded in raising the Order's spiritual fervor and apostolic zeal to the level of its first period, the reform returned the majority of priories to discipline and vigor. It was a renewed Order that faced the manifold developments that characterized the transition from medieval into modern times.

The attitude of the masters general and provincials toward reform was very important. They could weaken or strengthen the Observant movement, because the Conventuals controlled the government of the Order and provinces.* It was almost a hundred years before the Observants became strong enough to begin taking control of the administration.

Unlike Raymond of Capua, who inaugurated the reform movement, Thomas Paccaroni was little interested in it; Leonard Dati was too busy with the immediate concerns of ending the Schism and reuniting the divided Order. But Bartholomew Texier actively helped the reform and favored its leaders. His long, twenty-five-year term of office contributed materially to the growth of observance throughout the Order. Auribelli's attitude toward reform was not so much opposition as a fear that the growth of autonomous reformed congregations would destroy the Order's unity. Conrad of Asti was the first general drawn

---

*The labels, "Observant," applied to the reformed Dominicans and "Conventual," to the unreformed, are convenient terms borrowed from the Franciscans, among whom they have a more extensive meaning. The Franciscan nuances are too finely shaded to permit explanation here.

from the ranks of the Observants. Following Auribelli's second term, all the succeeding generals of the century were from the Congregation of Lombardy.

When the fifteenth century began, the reform movement stood on firm foundations in the priories of Colmar and Nuremberg, reformed in 1396, and in the monastery of Schönensteinbach, founded in 1397. Conrad of Prussia was vicar of these reformed communities. From them reform radiated in all directions during succeeding decades. South of the Alps, Clara of Gambacorta had established a fervent community of nuns in Pisa, and John Dominici, with the encouragement of Raymond of Capua, had taken the leadership of Observant friars and nuns in Venice. He organized new communities or returned older ones to fervor there and in surrounding cities. Under his direction the nuns of Corpus Christi Monastery, founded in 1392, soon became a model community. There was sound hope that from these beginnings the entire Order could be renewed by following the program of Raymond of Capua.

The reform reached outward as more priories embraced the primitive observance. Texier succeeded in introducing reform to the community of Basel. Antoninus became the first prior of San Marco, a house made famous by Fra Angelico and Savonarola, under whom it became the mother priory of a Congregation. Each reformed house became a center from which the Observance was propagated. Thus Basel reformed Vienna; from there reform spread into Hungary and Bohemia. Breslau became the leader in renewing the Polish province. Meanwhile the 1421 chapter, reviving the mandate of Raymond of Capua, ordered the provinces to found at least one priory of observance.

After the early leaders of the movement died, the masters general appointed vicars to guide the reform—Antoninus in central Italy, and Peter Geremia in Sicily. In Germany, Provincials Nicholas Nolten and Peter Wellen favored reform. In 1463 reform vicars took office in three vicariates, subdivisions of the province; then in 1465 a general vicar was appointed. By 1475 there were more reformed than unreformed priories, and the province elected an Observant provincial.

Because the unreformed Dominicans opposed and did much to

impede reform, Observant priories were forced to band together into congregations, which now become a regular feature of the Order's administration. Until then the only manifestation of the "congregation" had been the missionary Congregation of Pilgrim Friars. The first of the Observant groups was organized in Germany. Fearing a permanent division between Observants and Conventuals, like one that occurred among the Franciscans, the generals and provincials tended to be doubtful about the "congregations". Though opposed to them in principle, Auribelli was forced by circumstances to permit reformed groups to propose their own candidates for the vicars general. A new factor entered the picture with the formation of the autonomous congregation, having its own statutes, an elected vicar, and a chapter. It was a province within a province, nominally under the provincial, but exempt from his control in many respects. With minor variations, this became the pattern according to which larger congregations were organized. The Congregation of Lombardy, the first of the autonomous congregations, became a superprovince, enrolling priories of all the Italian provinces. Thomas of Lecco, vicar general in Lombardy, formed it with the approval of Pius II and the general chapter prodded Auribelli into giving it statutes in 1459. From 1464, the Congregation of Holland matched it. Holland's priories stretched across several provinces, from the Low Countries into France, and across Saxony into the Baltic region.

As the reform progressed, congregations were established in Spain, Aragon, Portugal, and France. Where a province had only a few reformed houses, they remained under the control of the provincial and a vicar appointed by him. Such was the case in Poland. The Congregation of San Marco, created by Savonarola in 1493 from priories detached from the Congregation of Lombardy, is the best known reformed group. Under its founder it followed an asceticism at variance with the Order's practices until Masters General Vincent Bandelli and Thomas de Vio Cajetan intervened. Although Alexander VI ordered the Congregation's dissolution in 1496, it did not disband. After Savonarola's execution, priories in Tuscany and, later, all the reformed houses of the Roman province were joined to it.

The Methods of Reform

The natural opposition of many of the Conventual friars to reform was intensified by some of the methods used by the Observants, who sought to advance their cause regardless of the cost. Isabella of Spain supported Alphonse of St. Cyprian, vicar in Castile, even when he tried to force reform on St. Stephen's at Salamanca and on Pena de Francia. He failed when the Salamancan community was able to show that its religious life was not lax, but stood at a good level of observance. Ten years passed before the priory voluntarily joined the reformed congregation. The Congregation of Holland attempted to seize and reform the priory of Antwerp and to annex the House of Studies at Louvain. Leonard Mansuetis had to restrain its vicar from disturbing the priories of Ypres, Bruges, and the monastery of Lille.

To curb the excessive zeal of the reformers, the masters and chapters penanced reformers who resorted to unjust methods and issued ordinances to protect the rights of the Conventuals. The popes stipulated that the consent of the majority of the community and of the master general or provincial had to be obtained before the reform could be introduced into any priory. The reform of a community usually entailed the departure, or, if brutal methods were used, the expulsion of the original inhabitants. Normally each friar was given the choice of remaining and accepting the reform or of searching for a community that would receive him. When Texier reformed Basel in 1429, he gave native friars the option of leaving or remaining but with some dispensations from the strictness of the new regime. Sooner or later most of them left.

The Observants soon discovered that a favorable public opinion and help of the civil and ecclesiastical authorities were indispensable for the successful reformation of a priory. Writing a guide for reformers about 1432, John Nider advised them to prepare the authorities and people and seek the support of influential priests and the bishop before attempting to introduce the Observance in any place. These by words, counsel, and approbation could influence both the religious and laity of the locality. Preachers should persuade the people to help the Observants, showing them the advantages of reform. Otherwise the unreformed would rally their parents, friends, and dignitaries to their cause. Ridiculing the whole idea of reform, they would predict dire consequences for the city, their friends, and themselves. History bears out the soundness of Nider's advice and the accuracy of his observations. When the people and the city were favorable to reform, it usually succeeded but when unfavorable, it invariably failed.

Discipline was at such a low level in many unreformed priories that kings, princes, and city governments readily lent support to reform attempts, or, as at Nuremberg in 1396, requested that a house be reformed. The succcess of the reform of all the Orders was so complete in Spain because Ferdinand and Isabella actively promoted it. At Lodi, in 1489, the people were so incensed at the spiritual and temporal ruin of their priory that they drove out the few friars who made up its community. In their anger they were about to tear the buildings down but an Observant friar persuaded them to stop. When the expelled community appealed to the master general, the angry citizens barred the doors against them.

Invariably observance was brought to a priory by colonies of reformed friars. Cardinal John Torquemada reformed Santa Maria sopra Minerva by importing Observant friars from Lombardy. A half century later, wanting to guarantee the continuance of reform at San Jacques in Paris, Thomas de Vio Cajetan curtailed the voting rights of unreformed friars and decreed that only an Observant might be elected prior there. The reform also progressed by making new foundations, sometimes near older houses which refused to undergo reform. Peter Geremia founded the Observant priory of St. Zita in Palermo in 1429, even though a priory dedicated to St. Dominic already stood in the city. Despite the conflicts that occasionally occurred, reformed and unreformed friars usually lived in fraternal amity, even though each side was jealous of its own position, rights, and privileges. If public opinion was against them, the Conventuals became less hostile toward their stricter confreres.

The advance of reform forced provincials to tighten observance in the unreformed priories, and as the century drew to a close, the Order began to reach into the ranks of the Observants for its provincials and generals. In 1505 Julius II asked that this practice become the rule for all superiors. Masters general and chapters were now solidly behind reform and began to prod slow-moving provincials to encourage reform more actively. Nor were they slow to recognize achievement. The 1498 chapter praised the provincial of Lombardy for his efforts in reforming Ferrara.

After the early opposition of the Conventuals subsided, they themselves tightened their discipline, forced by example and pressure from superiors. The gap between them and the Observants narrowed further as the reformers themselves, obliged by circumstances, became less strict in their interpretation of observances and more liberal in the use of dispensations. The times had altered radically since Dominic had developed the asceticism of his Order—its strict fasts and abstinence, its severe poverty. Two hundred years had passed and many observances that were within the reach of the average man of the thirteenth century exceeded the grasp of his fifteenth-century counterpart.

Raymond of Capua and the early leaders of the reform sought to restore the discipline of the Order's first century. When a priory accepted reform, the friars locked the gates and doors at a reasonable time at night, controlled admittance at all hours, restored cloister, fasts, perpetual abstinence, and silence, put poverty back on its pedestal, and required uniformity in living quarters and dress. They carried out Divine services with a dignity that won them God's blessing, the confidence of the people, and recruits and alms.

Despite all their good will, some observances became too much for them. Papal indults or dispensations from the master general permitted some priories to hold property or serve meat on certain days of the week. In 1465 Paul II granted the German province the privilege of eating meat once a day three times a week. Stating the reason for making the petition, Auribelli noted that Germany "was not a wine country and had a cold climate." Observant as well as Conventual houses benefitted by the grant. Three years later the Observant priory of Erfurt, in the province of Saxony, obtained the same privilege. As a house of studies it found the expense of providing wine, fish, and other abstinence-foods for a student body of about eighty friars too much for its budget. It faced the alternative of closing the school or going into debt. The reformed priories and monasteries of Portugal received permission from the master general in 1481 to eat meat on Sundays, Tuesdays, and Thursdays. The reasons ordinarily alleged in seeking the mitigation were poverty and the difficulty of supplying fish, eggs, and other substitute foods. Bl. Andrew Abellon, vicar of the Spanish reformed priories, provided "a solemn piece of beef and another of mutton," for the Feast of Holy Innocents. The strict law was enforced when no valid reasons existed for granting the petition.

Strict poverty also proved increasingly difficult even for the Observants. Master General Texier, an exponent of reform, was obliged to seek authority from Martin V in 1425 to permit individual priories, according to need, to acquire property and fixed revenues. When Antoninus, one of the leaders of the Observants, was prior at San Marco he judged it prudent to obtain an indult for it to hold possessions. Sixtus IV solved the impasse in 1475 when in reponse to the petition of Leonard Mansuetis, he granted the Order the right, in fact he obliged it, to acquire property. With one stroke he lifted the insupportable yoke of absolute poverty. The change freed the men from the incessant concern of finding the funds needed to sustain life and the ministry. It contributed greatly to the Dominican revival that was evident as the century closed. Among the Observants it was accompanied by a lessened severity that brought them and the Conventuals closer together.

Lacordaire and Père Mandonnet, an eminent Dominican historian of this century, accused the Observants of distorting the Order's spirit and Constitutions by suppressing the power of dispensation. This judgment does not stand critical examination. Some Observants, especially those of seventeenth-century France, did reject the dispensing power, but this was not true of Raymond's reform, or reform generally. Calling for the observance of the Constitutions to the letter, Raymond included the dispensing power, which stood at the head of the text. The Observants granted and used dispensations. However, knowing from history and experience how easily dispensations can be used irresponsibly and how often they end in laxity, they decided on a careful use of the dispensing power.

Mandonnet also charged that the Observants undervalued the Order's intellectual tradition. He was repeating a calumny that the opponents of the reformers first circulated. He added that the Observants produced no great doctors but directed their literary activity to moral and ascetical theology, history, and devotional subjects. He did not read his history carefully. The fifteenth century was deeply troubled and confused and needed that kind of literature. Moreover, Mandonnet forgot the careers of men like Francis Retz at the University of Vienna and Gerard Elten at Cologne. They were prominent doctors. It was from the ranks of the Observants that a new generation of Thomists arose in Cologne, Paris, and Italy toward the end of the century. Peter Crockaert in Paris, Francis of Vitoria in Spain, and Thomas de Vio Cajetan in Italy, all of them Observants, began their careers during the closing years of the fifteenth and achieved eminence in the next century. With the theologians of Cologne, they laid the foundations of the Thomistic revival which prepared the Order to meet the doctrinal onslaughts of Protestantism and make its contributions to the Council of Trent. Their works, carried forward by disciples, began a second golden age for Thomism. Together with Antoninus and Konrad Koellin of Cologne, they are of the same caliber as the theologians of the thirteenth and early fourteenth centuries.

Reform legislation limiting the number of friars who were promoted to degrees seems to be anti-intellectual. Yet it was precisely the inordinate ambition for degrees, rights and privileges that had created an excessive number of masters of theology, many of whom had not qualified or were of low caliber. The excessive privileges granted to masters of theology contributed mightily to decay. The Observants promoted enough men to the mastership to meet the needs of the schools under their control.

The reform movement was successful, though not completely so. It renewed enough priories to lay the groundwork for a revival of Dominican life during the 1400's and prepare the Order to enter the 1500's with new vigor and strength. It produced preachers, scholars, writers, friars, and nuns who have been canonized or beatified. Its preachers—John Dominici, Vincent Ferrer, John Nider, and Savonarola—rank with the best the Order has produced. Its scholars have already been mentioned. The unreformed friars can show nothing similar. Although there was a vocation-shortage in both Church and Order during the late decades of the century, the Observants often attracted recruits; the Conventuals had difficulty getting them. Enrolling hardly 30 friars when it accepted reform, Basel increased its community to 80 during the following years.

Raymond of Capua's program of reform was excellent. Seeking to renew the Order's life and ministry, he worked to lay a solid contemplative foundation, to create an environment of prayer and recollection sustained by community life, religious discipline, self-sacrifice, and constant study. As a holy man, the friend of St. Catherine, he knew from experience and observation that such a regime alone could evoke an apostolate in the mode that Dominic had fixed. He did not hesitate to establish stern standards or to turn for support to the popes, who gave it generously.

If the reformers might be criticized from the vantage point of several centuries, we might fault them for not reading the "signs of the times" with sufficient discernment, something we are not certain we are doing any better. This criticism seems to apply especially with regard to poverty. A millstone around the neck of the Order was an erroneous belief that Dominic had cursed anyone who would tamper with the poverty he had introduced. With the historical tools at hand, how could they have known that the curse was spurious? But if they had put aside legend for fact, they could have estimated the mind and temper of Dominic more rightly. Such a curse would have been totally out of keeping with his great spirit and predilection for collegiality. The lesson is clear. To read our times successfully, we need to listen to the Holy Spirit, know our history, understand our Founder, and go back to the sources and original inspiration of the Order. Nor should we neglect the wholesome traditions that developed through the centuries. Those who fear adaptation might reflect that every cherished tradition was once an innovation, at times a revolutionary one.

The reformers were handicapped by existing laws. They were forced to leave them behind when events proved to them that they could not turn the clock back to the days of Dominic. Recourse to sound principles of interpretation might have helped them sooner. The principle used by Peter de la Palu when Hugh of Vaucemain asked his opinion about poverty could have been applied. He held that strict observance could be mitigated when necessary and property held through an intelligent application of the dispensing powers. The unreformed certainly went too far in their neglect, but later generations approved some of the practical solutions they found for intolerable problems. To the point are the dispensations and indults that permitted even the Observants the use of meat on certain days of the week.

As the reform progressed, the strict views of John Dominici regarding poverty were replaced by the benign zeal of Antoninus, who clearly perceived that in many cases property was a necessity. Ultimately, Sixtus IV came to the rescue. His bull, attentive to the heart of the matter, safeguarded the substance of poverty. By permitting ownership he lifted from the Order the pressing burden of dire need, but left individual friars free to remain as poor as their conditions permitted. Had this accommodation to the times been made in the first quarter of the fourteenth century, it might have prevented the introduction of the private life, the wedge that opened the way to the abuses that proliferated after 1350.

These reflections fault our own renewal. Too much attention has been devoted to change, not enough to continuity. True progress, as John W. Gardner points out in his *Self-Renewal; The Individual and the Innovative Society,* is always a combination of both. Our vital spiritual and intellectual heritage must go on without interruption. This is continuity. Adaptation must be based on renewal of spirit. It must turn often to the sources and original inspiration that made our Order effective and great. The "signs of the times" cannot be discerned in a vacuum. If the reformers mistakenly tried to turn the clock back to "the good old days," we can make the more serious blunder of trying to wind a clock without a spring.

CHAPTER VII

THE SIXTEENTH CENTURY

The Order was strong when it entered the sixteenth century. Inner reform had reaffirmed its contemplative religious life, laid the foundations for a new period of productive intellectual activity, and rejuvenated its ministry. It was not as strong as it had been in the thirteenth century; it was older, not fully reformed, and its provinces in Bohemia, Hungary, and the Near East were extremely weak. Yet it was well prepared to face the new century and the onslaughts of Protestantism. The second period of Dominican history, stretching from 1500 to 1790, was beginning. Except for modifications of detail caused by forces beyond the Order's control—the Protestant Reformation, the Council of Trent, the trend toward absolute monarchy and nationalism, and many wars—Dominican life and ministry continued much as it had from 1215 to 1500.

The masters general during these centuries were sincere, earnest men, most of them from the ranks of the Observants. Some of them were men of personal holiness. Italy and Italian Dominicans dominated the Order until the French Revolution. Statistics demonstrate this fact. Of the 41 masters who governed from 1401 to 1798, only 13 were non-Italians; of the 68 general chapters held between 1462 and 1777 only 14 took place outside Italy and 33 outside Rome, a dominance that was legalized when the Order legislated in 1518 that chapters would meet alternately in Italy and beyond the Alps, a law largely nullified by convening all but 11 of the 47 chapters from then until 1777 in Italy—24 of the 26 elective chapters were held in Rome, the other two in Bologna. From 1252, when John of Wildenshausen died, until 1891, when Andrew Früwirth was elected, Spanish, French, and Italian Dominicans shared the generalate. During these centuries only Anthony Monroy, a Mexican Creole, broke this monopoly in 1677. Since 1891, three Spaniards, two Frenchmen, an Austrian, a German, and an Irishman have been master general. Added to these is Vincent de Couesnongle, a Frenchman, elected in August, 1974.

Since 1500, two Dominican popes, Pius V (1566-72) and Benedict XIII (1724-30), 41 cardinals, and more than 1,000 archbishops have served the Church. The master general and master of the sacred palace (a Dominican since the fifteenth century) functioned as *ex officio* consultors of the Holy Office (organized in 1542 and now the Congregation of the Faith). Its commissary was always a member of the Order, as was the secretary of the Index (abolished in 1917).

Government and Internal Life

Thirteen of the masters general of the century were Italians and all but three of the sixteen who held the office governed for short terms. After the five-year tenure of Vincent Bandelli (1501-06) and the two-month tenure of John Clerée (from June until August, 1507), Thomas de Vio Cajetan gave the Order ten years of strong and effective leadership, from 1508 to 1518. None of the next eight masters ruled for more than six years. Then Vincent Giustiniani had twelve years, (1558-70), Seraphim Cavalli, seven (1571-78), Paul Constabile, three (1580-82), and Sixtus Fabri, five (1583-89). Hippolite Beccaria closed the century. He held office for eleven years, from 1589 to 1600.

Despite the brevity of many of these terms, the masters moved continuously toward stronger and more personal rule, a trend that originated in the 1370's, when chapters stopped meeting annually. As the master's prestige grew, the functions of his curia kept pace, his assistants supplanting the general chapter as advisors.

The master's stronger position was balanced by more frequent interventions of the Holy See. The growing centralization within the Church that began with the Council of Trent and the establishment of new curial congregations, especially the Congregation for Consultations of Regulars in 1586, had a direct bearing on the Order. After the Congregation of Rites was established in 1588, and the Congregation of the Propagation of the Faith in 1622, the liturgy and foreign missions of the Order were subject to their jurisdiction. The Council of Trent subjected the preaching and sacramental ministries of religious to the supervision of the bishop by requiring priests to apply for permission to exercise these functions within his diocese.

The papal summoning of elective general chapters to Rome, which had begun in 1474, now became the rule. Frequently, too, the popes appointed the vicars general who governed during a vacancy in the generalate, passing over the vicar provided by the Constitutions. Leo X allowed Cajetan to function as general for almost a year after he made him cardinal in 1517. Sixtus Fabri fell victim to centralization, when Sixtus V deposed him in 1589, partly because of the opposition of Cardinal Michael Bonelli, Dominican nephew of Pius V, and partly because he had imprudently endorsed Sr. Marie of the Annunciation, a fraudulent mystic of the monastery in Lisbon.

The cardinal protectors regularly intervened in the Order's affairs. Though Sixtus IV sharply defined their powers in 1473, the century saw them acting at times as master of the Order. Bonelli served more than once as vicar general and proposed a slate of nominees for master in 1580. The protectors presided at elections of the master, signed the *acta* of chapters, dictated the appointment of provincials and priors, and received appeals. These interventions disrupted and obscured orderly constitutional administration.

The lesson of centralization was learned by the men of the Order. Acting on a mandate of Pius V, the 1569 general chapter restricted the appointment of all superiors to an aristocracy of prominent friars in each province, a subversion of the law that did not endure. But the example was not lost.

The masters and chapters of this century faced the challenge posed by the rise of Protestantism and bore the burden of implementing the decrees of the Council of Trent concerning religious. After religious strife became less violent, the masters resumed their periodic visitations of the provinces. Seraphim Cavalli visited in Italy, France, Spain, and the Spanish Netherlands. Sixtus Fabri spent two years visiting in Portugal and Spain.

The Order issued its first printed editions of the Constitutions in 1505 and 1507. Though the chapters thoroughly revised the Constitutions from 1515 to 1518, no new edition appeared until 1566. It incorporated changes made necessary by the decrees of Trent. A new feature, called the "minor text" is found in these editions. Under each heading of the Constitutions (now called the "major text") were gathered the enactments of general chapters which pertained to it. After the 1566 edition, the chapters seldom made changes in the major text. The Order was now governing itself as much by ordinances as by Constitutions, parts of which were kept in the text even after they became obsolete.

The Order began the century with twenty-two provinces and closed it with thirty-five. Though it lost Scandinavia and Scotland to Protestants and Palestine to the Turks, it erected new provinces in Italy, France, Spain, the Ukraine, nine in the Spanish colonial empire, and incorporated the Unifying Friars as the province of Naxivan. It founded the Congregation of the Holy Cross in the Asiatic possessions of Portugal in 1551.

Aided by the masters general, three of whom came from the Congregation of Lombardy, the Observants gained control of the Order. In 1515 Cajetan turned the Congregation of Holland into a province. Fifteen years later Butigella transferred the name and rights of the province of Rome to the Congregation of Tuscany. Du Feynier, his successor, permitted the Congregation of Lombardy to take control of the provinces of St. Dominic and St. Peter Martyr, the new names for the former provinces of Lombardy. In 1559, the Congregation of France became the province of Occitania. The Spanish province had completed its reform during the fifteenth century.

The Spiritual Life, the Sisters, and the Third Order

To strengthen Dominican internal life the 1505 chapter prescribed an annual retreat, a daily period of mental prayer, and the common recitation of the Rosary. In 1551 the Order revised its liturgy, publishing a new missal and breviary and, in

1576, a martyrology. After the canonization of Hyacinth and Raymond of Penyafort, their feasts were added to the liturgical calendar. Five saints lived during the century: Pope Pius V (d. 1572), John of Gorcum, martyred with eighteen non-Dominican companions in 1572, Catherine de Ricci (d. 1590), a member of the cloistered Third Order, Louis Bertrand (d. 1581), novice master and missionary, and Rose of Lima (d. 1617), a tertiary and the first canonized native of the New World. Sanctity also flourished among other members of the Dominican laity, notably Bartholomea Bagnesi (d. 1577) and Osanna of Cattaro (d. 1565) who have been beatified. A child of Orthodox parents in Dalmatia, Osanna dedicated her life to prayer for the reunion of the Churches. In Spain, Louisa Borgia (d. 1560), sister of St. Francis Borgia, was called the "Saintly Duchess".

The century was noted for the propagation of the Rosary and its Confraternity. The friars of Holland, Italy, and Spain were especially prominent in preaching the devotion. In 1521 Albert Castellano published an excellent Rosary book, one of the many that facilitated recitation and meditation on the mysteries, which Pius V standardized in their present form. He entrusted exclusive control of the Confraternity to the Order. Thomas of Nieto actively preached the newly introduced Forty Hours Devotion. To promote respect and veneration of the Eucharist, Thomas of Stella founded the first Blessed Sacrament Confraternity at Santa Maria sopra Minerva in 1539. In Spain, Diego of Vitoria preached devotion to the Holy Name.

Dominican nuns participated in the disasters and renewal of the Order. They suffered in Ireland, England, and Germany. Dartford in England and forty-three German monasteries fell before Protestantism. A great number of new foundations in Italy and Spain took their place. The nuns also entered the New World, establishing monasteries at Mexico City and Arequipa. As the century ended there were 206 monasteries, most of them in Italy, Spain, and Germany.

Studies and the Intellectual Mission

The Order continued to stress its intellectual ministry and

dedication to learning. Writing his first encyclical as general in 1508, Cajetan called on the friars to confirm their belief in study and poverty. He spoke as a distinguished scholar, whose contribution to the Thomistic revival had begun in the 1490's. He wrote the best commentary on the *Summa Theologiae*. Francis Silvester, who followed him in the generalate in 1525, penned the classical commentary on the *Summa Contra Gentiles*. Francis of Vitoria, the initiator of the Thomistic revival in Spain, was at the height of his career and pursued it to 1546, establishing at Salamanca a distinguished line of Thomists—Peter and Dominic de Soto, Melchior Cano, whose *De Locis Theologicis* elaborated a scientific theological methodology, and Dominic Banez, who contributed to the development of the theology of grace.

The theological authority of Thomas was further enhanced by the attention paid to his teaching at the Council of Trent, by Pius V's declaring him a Doctor of the Church in 1567, and the publication of the first complete printed edition of his works, the so-called *Piana* edition. From 1574 the Order required its theologians to take an oath to uphold his solid doctrine.

The Order's schools claimed the constant attention of the chapters. To the two graduate colleges for Thomistic studies in Luchente and Salamanca, founded late in the previous century, the Order added St. Gregory's in Valladolid in 1501, St. Thomas' in Seville in 1515, and St. Thomas' in Rome in 1577. This last is known today as the University of St. Thomas in Rome. A similar college was founded overseas in Santo Domingo in 1538. The traditional general houses of studies also continued. By 1551, their roster numbered twenty-seven, but those at Oxford and Cambridge and some in Germany had disappeared before advancing Protestantism. The one at Paris lost its pre-eminence as St. Stephen's in Salamanca rose to prominence under Vitoria.

Though the Order adapted its curriculum to the demands of the Renaissance and Protestantism slowly, Herman Rab, provincial of Saxony, pointed the way to change when he exhorted young friars to especially love "the science of Holy Writ." The provincial chapter of Saxony, a few years later, urged all its members to devote special attention to Scripture studies, so that they might effectively reply to Lutherans. Finally, in obedience to the decree of the Council of Trent, the Order introduced courses in biblical exegesis. The 1569 general chapter took a step backwards when it banned the works of Erasmus and similar writers and forbade friars to study Greek and Hebrew without permission. The 1585 chapter reversed this trend, ordering novices and newly professed religious to begin the study of languages before undertaking their formal academic training and to continue studying them for four years.

Except in Spain, Dominicans remained unalterable opponents of the Doctrine of the Immaculate Conception. Late in the century a new controversy, known as *De auxiliis*, broke out regarding the relationship of grace and free will. Theologians of the Thomist and Molinist schools debated the question with much acrimony until Paul V imposed silence on both parties in 1607, but allowed each school to continue teaching its own opinion.

Besides theologians and philosophers, other eminent scholars graced the Order during the century. Santes Pagnini was an accomplished Hebraist in an age that boasted Erasmus and Reuchlin. His books, translation of the Bible, Hebrew dictionary and grammar, biblical handbooks and commentaries form a miniature library of Oriental research. After Thomas de Vio Cajetan returned from his encounter with Luther at Augsburg in 1518, he began his translation of the Bible and commentary and wrote at least two-score treatises expounding points of doctrine attacked by Protestants. The *Bibliotheca Sacra* of Sixtus of Siena was based on scientific principles and is regarded as the first modern biblical introduction.

Other fields of interest also claimed Dominican attention. Applying Thomistic principles to contemporary ethical and economic problems, Francis of Vitoria laid the foundations of international law. Especially he and Melchior Cano were sensitive to humanistic and linguistic values in their works. John Faber of Augsburg made an abortive attempt to found a school of literary studies among his German brethren. Matthew Bandello is an example of the poor influence humanistic interest could exert on churchmen. Regarded as the leading Italian novelist of his day, he has been called the "Dominican Boccaccio." Zenobio Acciaioli, prefect of the Vatican Library under Leo X, and John Cono, a collaborator with Erasmus, were philologists; Ignatius Dante a mathematician, cosmographer, and engineer; Leander Alberti, Sebastian Olmeda, and Seraphim Razzi historians. Even today the *History* and controversial works of Bartholomew de las Casas are important for the study of social justice and race relations; the books of Louis of Grenada, for spiritual theology.

The Missions

Dominican missions reached their greatest development in modern times. Even before the end of the Middle Ages, Portuguese Dominicans rounded the Cape of Good Hope with navigators, founding missions in Africa, Goa (their headquarters), Ceylon, Siam, and Malacca. Their missions suffered from the British conquest of India but continued to flourish until the early nineteenth century. Gasper of the Holy Cross entered China in 1559.

In Spain, Archbishop Diego de Deza sponsored Christopher Columbus at the Spanish Court, who declared in 1504 that the Spanish sovereigns owed the Indies to de Deza. The first Dominican missionaries reached the West Indies in 1510 and founded the first American province in 1530. St. Louis Bertrand labored as a missionary in New Grenada from 1562 to 1569, enjoying the gift of tongues and miracles. Dominicans arrived in the Philippine Islands in 1586. From there they gained China in 1590.

The mission provinces boosted their membership by drawing friars from the Old World and by enlisting colonials born of European parents. Sharing the prejudices of their day, they failed to recruit Indians and people of mixed blood. The province of St. James in Mexico, which numbered 210 friars and 40 houses in 1555, illustrates the rapid growth of the American missions.

In the West Indies, Anthony Montesinos and Bernardino Minaya became the first defenders of the Indians. They were soon overshadowed by Bartholomew de las Casas, who carried the Indian cause to the Spanish Court. Though a classic source for the Spanish Colonial Period, his *Historia de las Indias* is marred by polemical bias in favor of the Indians. The *Relecciones de Indis* of Francis of Vitoria is a more scholarly treatment of the same problems. The Dominican, Jerome de Loaysa, first bishop of Lima, founded the University of Lima in 1551 and a hospital for the Indians. Dominic of St. Thomas compiled the first grammar for Quechua, the native Peruvian language.

The Dominicans and Protestantism

Protestantism swept like a tornado over the Order, damaging flourishing provinces, disrupting religious life, drying up vocations, and stripping away three provinces, forty-three monasteries, and many members. It washed over twelve provinces. Nine of them struggled back to their feet with great difficulty. Germany was making a good recovery in 1618 when it was again beaten down by the destruction of the Thirty Years War. Hungary, already weakened by the Turks, and Bohemia, gravely damaged by the Hussites, were so badly hurt by Protestantism that they needed several centuries to regain strength. Persecution hammered at Ireland until the nineteenth century. England became strong again only in the twentieth. The Saxon province was so seriously mauled that it was reduced to seven priories. It went out of existence when these were united to the German province in 1608. Scandinavia and Scotland disappeared by mid-century.

With the weakening of the non-Latin provinces, the tone of the Order altered. The Italian, French, and Spanish friars now dominated the Order. The moderating influence of other peoples was lost until the twentieth century.

German Dominicans were the first to take the field against Luther. John Tetzel, who had triggered the explosion when he preached indulgences, his Saxon brethren, the Master of the Sacred Palace, and Cajetan wrote the first literary rebuttals. In 1525 Clement VII urged the electors assembled in chapter to choose a new master general, to put aside all personal motives and ambition and elect "a man pre-eminent in doctrine," one who could guide the Order to the fulfillment of its customary mission "during times brimming over with danger and anxiety." He could not have been disappointed in the choice, Francis Sylvester, the Thomistic commentator. The general and provincial chapters repeatedly warned friars against preaching and teaching old or new errors, urged them to proclaim true doctrine, exhorted provincials to concentrate learned, zealous men in priories near Protestant areas, and to counsel the master general how Dominicans could best work for the conversion of their people. They were to specify men who were able to preach, teach, and debate with non-Catholics.

The legislators in 1523, 1525, and 1530 invoked the memory of the Order's great men who had studied, prayed, and rooted out harmful doctrines, and had been ready to resist unto blood, running joyfully toward death. Such talk was not idle. The words of encouragement chapters sent from time to time to embattled provinces were matched by lists of nuns and friars who had died for the faith. The 1580 chapter listed martyrs in Germany, Holland, and France.

There were also many Dominican men and women who left the Order and the Church. Best known is Martin Bucer, one of the leading Reformers in Germany and England. Following his example most of the friars at Strassburg had married by 1526.

Dominican preachers, theologians, and writers turned with a will to the proclamation of the word of God and its defense. Tacchi Venturi, the Jesuit historian, states that "Dominicans ran well ahead of other Catholic defenders in point of time, numbers, and excellence of doctrine." Studying the Dominican counterattack on Lutheranism, Nicholas Paulus concluded that "no other religious Order produced so many outstanding literary champions as the Order of St. Dominic." In Italy, fourteen of sixty-four literary opponents of Protestantism were Dominicans. Melchior of Misciska, an outstanding preacher, is credited with the return of 22,000 Polish Protestants to the Church. We need not detail the work of the Order's papal nuncios in Germany, of inquisitors in France and Italy, or of Spanish friars who helped to rehabilitate other provinces.

In reviewing the Dominican reaction to Protestantism, we might well reflect on the dictum of a church historian that polemic between Catholics and Protestants has been largely ineffective. For three centuries each side lobbed its shells—books, treatises, and rebuttals—at the other. They seldom reached their mark, but each camp was extremely pleased with itself. Only today have the two armies put aside their weapons and begun to talk. The entry of Dominicans into ecumenical dialogue accords perfectly with the Order's mission to proclaim the word of God throughout the world.

Ecclesiastical Ministry

Dominicans helped the Church in the sixteenth century, by entering the hierarchy, serving as legates and inquisitors, and attending general councils. At the Fifth Lateran Council, Cajetan defended both the primacy of the pope and the rights and privileges of mendicant Orders.

The Order made a major contribution to the Council of Trent, the assembly that restated Catholic doctrine, gave direction and impetus to Christian life and reformed the Church. Two hundred Dominicans contributed as archbishops and bishops, deputies of bishops, theologians, or, as the three Portuguese friars, delegates of their king. Great Dominican names took part in the deliberations of the Council's three periods: Dominic de Soto, Bartholomew Carranza, Ambrose Politus Cathrinus, Melchior Cano, Peter de Soto, Ambrose Pelargus, Peter of Bertano, bishop of Fano, Bartholomew of the Martyrs, archbishop of Braga, and Masters General Francis Romeo and Vincent Giustiniani. Thomas Aquinas was there in spirit. Preaching to the fathers in 1563 John Gallo claimed that "no council has been celebrated without this holy doctor" since the Council of Lyons. "Consider your own assembly... consulted most frequently in the most learned congregation of fathers, this doctor expresses his opinion. By common consent you referred any ambiguity or controversy that arose to him as to the touchstone." Yet the Council endorsed no theologian or school. It consulted a multitude of authorities and heard the views of every theological school. Perhaps the place of Thomas at the Council was best stated by Louis von Pastor, the historian of the popes, who wrote, "The Church recognized her own doctrines in those of the great schoolman."

The age-old distrust of the exemption and privileges of the mendicant Orders came to a head at the Council. Had not able defenders spoken in their behalf, the bishops would have reduced the Orders to dependence on themselves. Instead, the assembly adapted the mendicants to the new age, modified their exemption and privileges, brought their preaching and sacramental ministries under episcopal supervision and provided wise laws for the discipline and life of the Orders. Once again, an important arm of the Church was not weakened but strengthened.

That the work of the Council did not remain a dead letter was due to Pius IV and especially to Pius V. His well-worn copy of the decrees illustrates how faithfully he applied them during his six-year pontificate. In the diocese of Braga, Archbishop Bartholomew of the Martyrs exemplified the ideal bishop envisioned by the Council. Charles Borromeo patterned himself on the saintly Archbishop. Dominicans served on the post-conciliar commissions that prepared the *Catechism of the Council of Trent,* the *Index of Forbidden Books,* and the renewal of the liturgy. Pius V published the revised missal and breviary that unified the Roman Rite.

Dominicans also served the Church by helping founders of new Orders: Anthony Maria Zaccaria of the Barnabites, Jerome Niani of the Somaschi, Philip Neri of the Oratorians, and Ignatius Loyola of the Society of Jesus during his retirement at Manresa. Teresa of Avila of the Discalced Carmelites received encouragement from several Dominican confessors and advisors.

CHAPTER VIII

THE SEVENTEENTH CENTURY, AN AGE OF ABSOLUTISM

The Order entered this century with strength and vigor. It shared the restoration of Catholic life that followed the Council of Trent. The Dominican reform movement had come to substantial completion, a series of great theologians had brought about a Thomistic revival, and the core provinces in Italy, Spain, and France were sound and became ever more thriving and populous. This strength was matched by weakness. The provinces of northern and eastern Europe were but shells; the provinces overseas were strong but too distant and too absorbed in the ministry to exert much influence in the Order; the intellectual revival had spent most of its strength, and controversies were claiming the energy that theologians might have used more effectively.

In the political world, Divine Right Monarchy, nationalism, and dynastic wars were about to begin. Catholic princes would soon restrict the liberty of the Church, challenge papal leadership, and sap the strength of the religious Orders. As Philip Hughes has written, "In the long run the absolutism of Catholic princes was to ruin the influence of Catholicism in the south as truly as the Protestants had ruined it in the north, and to inflict injuries on religion that are still felt as a real hindrance." Religious Orders, too, were caught in the web that entangled the Church. It was no accident that "the movements that made life so difficult for the Church between 1600 and 1800 originated in France; absolutism, Gallicanism, Jansenism, episcopalism," and the French Revolution. Assisted by Cardinals Mazarin and Richelieu, the Bourbon dynasty, which succeeded to the French throne in 1594, carried royal power to such a pitch that Louis XIV became the incarnation of the "Divine Right King". Richelieu's policy of limiting papal authority in France to the degree compatible with orthodoxy became dogma and received classic expression when Louis promulgated the Gallican Articles in 1682.

In the Church, the concentration of powers in the papacy that began after the Council of Trent developed as the papal position strengthened. Necessary and salutary in the sixteenth century, when the decrees of Trent needed to be implemented and Catholic reform was still in its infancy, Roman control was destined to be challenged once the restoration of Catholic life had been accomplished and royal powers and episcopal prerogatives were more vigorously asserted.

Dominican Government, Its Changing Character

Absolutism, centralized government, and Rationalism reached their peak in the "enlightened" eighteenth century. The Order was touched by all of them and found its freedom of action curtailed by frequent papal and royal interventions. Nor could it break free of its times or escape the entanglements of papal and dynastic policies. A proposal of Master General Beccaria in 1600 to entrust the appointment of provincials to the master was prophetic of the changing atmosphere in the Order itself. The centralization and pomp that encompassed it on every side entered its own blood stream. The dominance of the master general, which began when general chapters stopped meeting annually in 1370, developed into a kind of monarchy during the seventeenth and eighteenth centuries. Until 1622 the chapters convened more or less regularly at three-year intervals. Three years later, Urban VIII authorized meetings at six-year intervals. The interim tended to be much longer. A chapter took place in 1628 and another in 1629 to elect a general, but then the fifteen that met until 1832, with four exceptions, assembled only to elect. Innocent XI attempted to change this situation in 1677, requiring the return to triennial chapters, but his order remained a dead letter. The chapter came together only six times during the eighteenth century.

The influence of the master increased accordingly. Reaffirming its authority and that of the master, "who holds the plenitude of power through the Order both in spirituals and temporals," the general chapter of 1600 reserved to him and the diffinitors the title "Most Reverend." At the same time, it obliged the master to reside in Rome, a sign that his increasing importance was lessening his personal contact with the provinces. He kept in touch through letters, executive orders, grants of dispensation and privileges, adjudication of disciplinary cases, hearing of appeals, and occasional visitations, made either by himself or delegates. The infrequency of chapters obliged him, from time to time, to have recourse to the Holy See for authorizations or decisions. Nor could the provinces resist the thrust toward personal rule. The 1629 general chapter found it necessary to command the diffinitors of the provincial chapter not to empower the provincial to change the *acta* of chapters. The 1647 general chapter increased the master's control by ordering that the *acta* of provincial chapters be submitted to him for review before promulgation.

The power of the master was symbolized in many ways. New construction at his headquarters, Santa Maria sopra Minerva, made the priory a massive complex that housed the master and his curia, the administration of the Roman province, St. Thomas College and its professors, and, in the next century, the scholars and professors of the Casanate Library. Also, forced by circumstances to remain at the heart of the Church, the masters provided a summer house for themselves in the countryside near Palestrina. Marinis was the first to go there in 1656 because of weakened health, but the generalate bought the home, and the masters used it regularly from about 1677. There they placed real or fabricated portraits of their predecessors. This gallery, kept up-to-date, now hangs in the master's corridor at Santa Sabina. This is a forgivable piece of family pride. Though the portraits are imaginary before the seventeenth century, great men like Dominic, Jordan, Humbert, Raymond of Capua, and Cajetan deserve to be commemorated.

The pomp and splendor reserved to princes were not wanting, especially when the Order elected the sons of aristocratic families: John Thomas Rocaberti in 1670, Anthony Monroy in 1677, John Thomas Boxadors in 1756. Since 1669, probably, Spanish kings have honored the master as a Grandee of Spain. Baroque pomp and circumstance attended the visitation tour of Antoninus Cloche to upper Italy. Though the personal life of Boxadors was characterized by simplicity and great austerity, his four-year visitation of the Spanish provinces, begun in 1760, provoked the accusation that he had traveled like a prince. Elections and funerals often became the occasion of splendor and show. The municipal band of Rome, not without suitable gratuitees, of course, beat their drums and blew their trumpets to herald the election of Augustine Pipia in 1721. Great numbers of Dominicans, and many religious and ecclesiastical dignitaries graced the funerals of Cloche in 1720 and Ripoll in 1747.

Though the master's position was stronger, neither he nor the Order could function in full freedom. By 1600 close supervision by the pope and cardinal protector was well established. All fourteen of the elective chapters of the seventeenth and eighteenth centuries voted under the watchful eye of the Holy See. Also, the pope regularly appointed a vicar general to govern the Order during a vacancy. So appointed were Ridolfi in 1628 and 1650, Vincent Candido in 1644, and Pius Passerini in 1670. The popes also continued a precedent established a century earlier by retaining the master general in office (pending the election of a successor) after his elevation to the hierarchy—Augustine Galamini to the cardinalate, 1611, Rocaberti to the archbishopric of Valencia (1677), Monroy to that of Compostella (1685), and Boxadors to the cardinalate in 1775. Cardinal Fausto Poli presided over the sessions of the 1644 elective chapter. By a grant of Urban VIII, the vicar general, Vincent Candido, cast a vote even though he was not a capitular. Holding the Order's well being at heart, the Holy See also sent directives to the chapters from time to time. Cardinal Altieri, the protector, obliged the 1677 elective chapter to accept several mandates before proceeding to the election—that the Order hold triennial chapters, observe the procedure approved by Boniface IX when promoting to the mastership in theology, and not alter the Constitutions or acts of the chapters. Furthermore, the master general was to visit all the European provinces personally. The cardinal also commanded the chapter, after the election, to appoint a commission to revise the Constitutions. Cloche published this revision in 1690. Preceded by the editions of 1620 and 1650, it was printed and reprinted without alteration until Jandel promulgated the edition of 1872.

The new insistence on visitations by the master proved to be futile. Earlier in the century the pope had prevented Ridolfi, Marinis, and Rocaberti from making visitations. Now circumstances stood in the way. Making a visitation in upper Italy, Cloche, a Frenchman, was barred by Spain from entering the Duchy of Milan or visiting the Spanish provinces. For the sake of peace, he did not go to France.

Another sign of the times was the position of privileges and exaggerated respect accorded to masters of theology. An extreme example is afforded by an ordinance of the 1649 provincial chapter of Aragon: "Because the masters bring great honor to the Order by their literary productions, we wish them to have complete freedom to work. That is why we order . . . priors to designate lay brothers who shall carefully and humbly serve them." The eminent station of the masters was aggrandized by their predominance at the general chapters, which began in the fifteenth century, and by the extended body of privileges they enjoyed. These facts lie behind the puzzling reference of Charles Poulet in his *Church History* to "the division of the Dominican Order into a high and low clergy." The masters pushed the preachers general into the shadows, even though the latter continued to be members of the provincial chapters.

The Seventeenth-Century Masters General

Nine masters ruled during the 1600's. Five of them had tenures of seven years, none had less than four. Seraphim Secci (1612-1628), Nicholas Ridolfi (1629-1644), John Baptist Marinis (1650-1669), and Antoninus Cloche enjoyed lengthy terms. The thirty-four-year term of Cloche, the most long-lived of the masters, linked two centuries. Elected in 1686, he died in 1720. The generalship of Jerome Xavierre (1601-1607), marked a brief interlude in the long series of Italian masters. Another interruption came at the end of the century with the elections of Thomas Rocaberti, a Spaniard (1670-77), Anthony Monroy, a forty-two-year-old

Mexican Creole (1677-86), and Cloche, a Frenchman.

Ridolfi shared the fate of Munio Zamora, Martial Auribelli, and Sixtus Fabri. Urban VIII turned him out of office after some of his own friars had trumped up charges against him and made an illegal attempt to depose him at an irregular chapter held at Genoa in 1642. This provoked a schism, a protest general chapter at Corneliano near Genoa, and the election of two pseudo-generals, one of them the ambitious Michael Mazarin, brother of the famous Cardinal. Later he too donned the red hat. Urban VIII, who had suspended Ridolfi, nullified both illegal chapters and elections in 1643 and removed Ridolfi in 1644. He and his cardinal-nephews, who had encouraged the enemies of the master, had family reasons for detesting Ridolfi. He was rehabilitated by Urban's successor, Innocent X, who named him president of the chapter assembled in 1650 to elect a successor to Thomas Turco (1644-1649). He would probably have been re-elected but death cut him down as he was reaching for the fruit of victory.

The Chapters and the Provinces

The general chapters of the century busied themselves with their traditional work, providing for the well being of the Order, provinces, studies, and regular discipline. The 1605 chapter, especially, issued a series of decrees dealing with reform. The 1611 chapter, assembled in Paris, was marked by the anti-Gallican debates that were held in the presence of Marie de Medici, Queen Regent, the youthful Louis XIII, the papal nuncio and members of the nobility. Several times during the century, chapters had to emphasize the unity of the Order in the face of attempts to appoint a vicar general for the provinces of the Indies and the introduction of novelties regarding the habit and ceremonies. Despite these efforts, the capuce and its hood greatly increased in fulness, their ample cut enduring well into the nineteenth century. To distinguish themselves from other friars who walked bareheaded or wore skullcaps, Dominicans began to wear the Roman hat in public.

Changes in the government of the provinces were introduced

by the general chapter of 1629. In conformity with decrees of Julius II, that had been implemented only in Italy, the Order now fixed the duration in office of provincials at four years, and of priors at three years. In line with this change, provincial chapters would meet only to elect a provincial, at four-year intervals. In between chapters, selected fathers of the province, masters of theology, and priors were to meet to discuss the affairs of the province. This assembly would have no elective or legislative powers. Some of the provinces adopted customs of their own. Aragon and Calabria chose their provincials in rotation from the various vicariates of the province. The Mexican Dominicans alternated between a Spanish and a creole provincial. The province also divided itself into regions depending on the language spoken by the natives, whether Mixtec or Zapotec.

From the Protestant Reformation until the French Revolution, the greatest strength of the Order lay in Italy, Spain, and France. The French provinces suffered greatly from the foreign invasions and protracted civil and religious wars that had troubled France in the sixteenth century. Benefiting from the creation of reformed congregations and provinces and the revival of Catholic life that began in France with the belated implementation of the decrees of Trent, the French friars, until then in need of reform, recovered during the 1600's. Bohemia and Hungary remained extremely weak and recovered only slowly from the blows inflicted by the Protestants and the Turks. The German province was making a good recovery when the Thirty Years War, which began in 1618, again weakened it. The Turks destroyed the province of Greece in 1669. The Order itself put an end to the province of Saxony in 1608, uniting its few houses to the German province. It added nine new provinces to its roster: Piedmont, St. Catherine's in southern Italy, Paris, Lithuania, the Canary Islands, Holy Angels in Mexico, St. Louis in France, Belgium, and St. Hyacinth's in Russia.

Political pressures dictated some of this realignment of the Order's territory. To accord with civil jurisdictions, kings had the boundaries of provinces shuffled or priories gathered into autonomous congregations. The Order itself established the Congregation of Sardinia, dividing it from the Aragonese province in 1615. Influenced by the Habsburgs, it carved the Congregation of Steiermark and Carinthia from the German province in 1629. The conquests of Louis XIV led to the erection of a French-speaking province of Belgium in 1680 and the Congregation of Alsace in 1690. Malta with its three priories became a vicar-generalate after the island passed under British control. On the other hand, in 1605, the Order suppressed the Congregation of Silesia, established after the partition of Poland, by reuniting its four priories to the province of Poland. The Order's reform movement accounted for the erection of another nine congregations in Italy, France, and Russia.

The level of Dominican life in the provinces and congregations varied greatly. The northern provinces were caught in the meshes of the Protestant environment or held back by the century's dynastic ambitions and wars. The zeal of the French Dominicans for reform led them into a certain instability and discontent, manifested in the multiplication of congregations and the shifting of provincial boundaries. The Spanish and Italian provinces were living and vital. Lombardy had 2,033 friars and 63 houses; the Sicilian province, 800 friars (1573); the province of Spain, 2,000; Aragon, 1,152 in fifty-three priories. The ten provinces of the Spanish colonies were moderate-sized. At its establishment in 1656, Holy Angels province in Mexico had nineteen priories.

The Reform Movement

The masters general actively promoted the Order's reform during this century. Xavierre guided the reforming chapter at Valladolid in 1605. Secci, himself an exemplary religious, conducted frequent visitations personally or through visitators. Turco spent 1645 and 1646 in France bringing order into the confused picture of reformed provinces and congregations. He then went into Spain. Two of the reformed congregations of France achieved provincial rank in 1669, the Gallican under the title, province of Paris, and the congregation of St. Louis, which kept the same name. In response to a directive of the Congregation of Regulars, sent to the chapter that elected him in 1677,

Monroy and the capitulars framed wise ordinances for the reintroduction of the common life in the Order's priories. In most of them a greater or lesser degree of private life (a failure to share all things) was in effect.

This constant concern for reform was necessary, for the reason just mentioned and also because pockets of unreformed friars continued to exist and Observants themselves experienced periods of decline. The 1605 general chapter returned to Raymond of Capua's plan, demanding that one priory of observance be established in each province. The French Dominicans went a step further in 1629, setting up a general novitiate at Paris, at the prompting of Ridolfi. A 1652 decree of Innocent X unfortunately was not well implemented. He directed all Orders to suppress small religious houses, which experience had shown could not maintain religious discipline.

Studies

The Order strengthened its program of studies in obedience to Tridentine decrees and papal directives. Turning their attention to theology, the general chapters introduced practical moral courses to the curriculum, dividing students into "formal" and "material." "Formal" students were eligible for degrees and concentrated on studying the works of Thomas Aquinas. More important still, the chapters punctuated the century with directives providing for increased study of the Bible in the houses of studies and principal priories, the appointment of professors of the Scriptures, daily biblical lectures to accompany the four-year course of theology, and, in 1694, the opening of a school of biblical studies in each province. This concern for the Scriptures was extended to the original languages. The 1608 chapter took the first step, requiring the provinces to establish a Greek and Hebrew language school. A 1622 mandate obliged the provinces to institute courses in Hebrew, Greek, Latin, and Arabic in all the houses of philosophy and theology. Though the lack of skilled linguists probably made obedience to these orders difficult, they did bear fruit in the work of several scholars. Francis Combefis prepared pioneer editions of the Greek Fathers. In his *Eucho-*

logium, Jacques Goar described the Oriental Rites in a manner that was unsurpassed at that time. Michael le Quien authored the important *Oriens Christianus.* John Michael Vansleb published a lexicon of the Ethiopian language.

The general chapters frequently reminded the friars of the Order's doctrinal mission and their duty to develop and maintain the Thomistic heritage. To this end Colleges were established at Bogotá in 1612 and in Quito in 1681. The province of the Holy Rosary established the University of Santo Tomás, Manila, in 1645. The previous year the general chapter had called for the publication of the works of the great Dominican masters. Accordingly, the writings of Albert the Great, Thomas Aquinas, and the *Commentary* of Peter of Tarentaise on the *Sentences* were published at mid-century. Outstanding Thomistic scholars were Thomas Lemos, John of St. Thomas, noted for his theological and philosophical commentaries, John Baptist Gonet, Jerome Medici, Vincent Contenson, and Anthony Goudin.

Seventeenth-century Thomists inherited the long-standing controversy over the Immaculate Conception and the dispute with the Molinists over grace and free will. New problems arose and continued into the eighteenth century—those connected with Jansenism, Probabilism (a method for solving cases of conscience), and Gallicanism. Dominicans were forced to walk a tight rope between the opinions of the Jansenists and the probabilism of the Jesuits. They challenged both adversaries, who themselves warred with each other. When Thomists expounded their views on grace, they seemed to be teaching Jansenism; when they attacked the laxity of some probabilists, they risked being identified with the extremely severe disciplinary and sacramental tenets of the Jansenists. Ironically, a Spanish Dominican, Bartholomew Media, originated Probabilism in 1577. Several other Dominican theologians adopted the system, but because of the abuses it occasioned, the 1656 general chapter condemned it. Two subsequent condemnations by Pope Alexander VII, a decree of Innocent XI, and other official statements supported Dominicans in their opposition to Probabilism.

The Gallican controversy did not directly involve the Order. Nevertheless, King Louis XIV's imposition of the anti-papal

Gallican Articles in 1682, requiring professors of theology and candidates for degrees to accept them, bore heavily on the French Dominicans. The Articles remained legally binding but were not enforced after the conflict that erupted between Louis and the Pope was settled in 1693. Master General Rocaberti reacted sharply against Dominicans who became Gallicanists. He rebuked Noel Alexander, the celebrated theologian and church historian, for his anti-Roman attitude and himself took up the pen in defense of papal rights. Alexander was not alone in his enthusiasm for the French position. John Carée, an extremely patriotic and somewhat fanatical Dominican Observant, took a vow of obedience to Cardinal Richelieu, one of the architects of Gallicanism. However, as time passed most of the friars went over to the papal side.

The Order took no official note of the Enlightenment, the movement arising from the philosophical systems of the seventeenth century. Most Scholastic philosophers and theologians failed to respond to the philosophical challenges of the Enlightenment and went into an intellectual ghetto. However, many individual Dominicans developed a scholarship attuned to the times. Thomas Campanella, who preceded Descartes in positing a universal methodic doubt at the beginning of his system, was renowned for the boldness of his ideas, his philosophical and theological ideas, and his tragic life. The *Icones plantarum* of Jacques Barelier, based on the personal observations of the author, dealt with the plant life of France, Spain, and Italy. It is one of the foremost botanical works of the century. Like many men of the early modern period, Ignatius Dante excelled in several fields. An architect, mathematician, cosmographer, and astronomer, he authored a number of scientific writings. Vincent Maculano, who also became a cardinal, was an engineer of note. Commissioned by Urban VIII, he constructed the fortifications of Malta and strengthened those of Rome. A number of Dominican historians wrote during the century, notably Alphonse Chacon, Jean de Rechac, Abraham Bzowski, James Quétif, Thomas Souèges, and Noel Alexander. They devoted themselves to Dominican or ecclesiastical history. At the urging of Chacon, Master General Xavierre began to encourage study of history in the Order. Marinis greatly enlarged the Order's archives at the Minerva during his generalate. Quétif, a literary historian, launched his monumental *Scriptores ordinis Praedicatorum*, a history of Dominican writers that James Échard completed in 1754. Souèges published a multivolumed collection of biographies of Dominican men and women. In his *Historia ecclesiastica*, a collection of 230 historical monographs, Noel Alexander manifested a true sense of history. Literary pursuits appealed also to some of the Order's nuns. Flammette Frescobaldi, a Florentine, was a chronicler. Plautina Nelli, another Florentine, and Violanta de Ceo, a Portuguese, wrote poetry. They were joined by Diego Ojeda, when he published his *Christiade* in 1611. Ignatius Nente deserves mention as the author of the first treatment of devotion to the Sacred Heart.

Preaching and the Missions

As in other centuries, the preaching of the Order went largely unrecorded during the seventeenth. Testimony to the continuing consciousness of its mission are the regulations issued by Secchi in 1612 to stimulate preaching, the establishment of quotas in 1644 and 1650 of the number of missionaries who might be promoted to the preacher-generalship, and the ordinances of 1677. These last envisioned a return to the primitive mission of the Order, a purpose that had receded into the background when friars became degree-conscious, and masters and bachelors disdained to do popular preaching. The ordinances, which happily did not remain a dead letter, called on "men of zeal, religion, doctrine, and eloquence" to preach popular missions. Vincent de Paul had grasped the need for this when he founded the Vincentians, who would soon be imitated by the societies of priests founded by Louis Grignion de Montfort, a Dominican tertiary, and Alphonse Liguori.

The following examples indicate the kind of special preaching Dominicans were doing. Working in Venice, Xantes Mariales attacked prevailing abuses so vehemently that the irate citizens drove him out of the city. Timothy Ricci was reputed to have drawn 30,000 people to his sermons in Bologna. He also introduced choral recitation of the Rosary and developed the devotion of the perpetual Rosary to ensure round-the-clock recitation. Dominicans in Belgium, Holland, and France continually battled the Jansenists. Flemish friars evangelized in the Protestant states of Denmark, Holstein, and Hamburg from 1623 to 1639. A few Scottish seminarians who became Dominicans in Rome returned home to work as missionaries. Bishop Coiffeteau took the pulpit against the Calvinists of Metz and Marseilles. From the sixteenth century to 1847, preaching to the Jewish people of Rome was entrusted to the Order.

The missions of the New World were staffed by creole friars and recruits from Spain. The province of the Holy Rosary, founded in 1592, drew its friars from Spain, trained them there, and sent them to the Philippines, China, Japan, and Indochina. The Portuguese friars manned missions in Mozambique, India, and the Moluccas. The Peruvian province produced three examples of exceptional sanctity: St. Rose of Lima, St. Martin de Porres, and Bl. John Massias. French Dominicans entered the islands of Guadaloupe and Martinique after 1625. The Italians supplied the membership of the Congregation of the Orient, the new name of the Pilgrim Friars. They maintained stations in the Pera suburb of Constantinople, Smyrna, Crimea, and Greater Armenia.

In China, Dominicans became involved in the Chinese Rites controversy that arose from the methods of Matteo Ricci, head of the Jesuit missionaries, who permitted converts to continue their ancestral customs and to pay honor to Confucius. Opposed by Dominicans, Augustinians, and some Jesuits, Ricci's methods led to a century-long debate. In the 1700's the Holy See banned the use of the Rites by Christians, judging that it was impossible, given the tone of Chinese society at that time, to separate superstitious elements from their practice. The changed complexion of Chinese civilization led to a lifting of the prohibition in the early twentieth century.

The Church drew ten cardinals from the Order's ranks during the 1600's. The century was also rich in Dominicans who suffered for the Faith. The Japanese beheaded Bl. Alphonse Navarette in 1617 and the Chinese, Bl. Francis Capillas, the protomartyr of their land, in 1649. Europe also produced martyrs. Many Dominicans gave their lives during the Tartar invasions of Ruthenia in 1648-1649. All during the century, the friars of Ireland, Scotland, and England suffered harassment, imprisonment, and sometimes death. The Irish province offered a holocaust of over 100 martyrs and many deportees. Some English friars spent long years in prison. Venerable Robert Nutter was hanged, drawn, and quartered at Lancaster in 1600. David Joseph Kemeys died in Newgate prison, London, in 1680, and Patrick Primrose paid for his zeal by death in a Scottish prison in 1670. Preceded by Anthony Temmerman, who died in 1582 rather than betray the secrets of the confessional, the Dominicans of Holland endured fines, imprisonment, and expulsion. Father Steur and Henry Wildeman were severely beaten by soldiers.

During the 1700's the inner life of the Order was promoted by the addition of the feasts of five newly canonized Dominicans to the liturgical calendar, the publication of new editions of liturgical books, and increased devotion to St. Dominic and St. Thomas. The Vatican placed the statue of St. Dominic in St. Peter's basilica; the Order venerated him by introducing the Fifteen Tuesdays devotion in his honor and by decorating his tomb-chapel with the *Glorification of St. Dominic*, painted by Guido Reni. Piedmontese and Belgian Dominicans commemorated the purity of Thomas by introducing the Confraternity of the St. Thomas Cord.

Beginning with this century, a nationalism that has not yet died completely began to blemish the fraternal life of the Order. This development was probably inescapable at a time when French, Spanish, and Italian Dominicans dominated the Order, and when provinces were being created and boundary lines redrawn to satisfy kings who could not endure having their subjects render obedience to an alien religious or princely superior. The return to the collegiality and subsidiarity of the Order's earlier centuries and the abolition of all privileged offices and votes, steps that were taken in 1968, provide better standards than nationality and privilege for estimating the dignity of a person.

CHAPTER IX

THE EIGHTEENTH CENTURY UNTIL 1789

The seventeenth century merged into the eighteenth as imperceptibly as summer blends into autumn. The century reaped what the 1600's had sown and, at its end, it reaped a hurricane. The French Revolution broke over Europe with hurricane force in 1789 and swept away the Old Regime—an order of society that was hoary with age and full of dry rot. The Dominican Order found the transition into autumn just as easy. Its master general, Antoninus Cloche, who had held the reins since 1686, ushered it peacefully into the new century. He could hardly have suspected, when he died an old man of ninety-two in 1720, that the Order, glorious like the monarchy of Louis XIV, would be weak, broken, and lying prostrate when his fifth, eighteenth-century successor, Balthasar Quinones, died in 1798. Between the two came Augustine Pipia, Thomas Ripoll, Antoninus Bremond, and John Thomas Boxadors. Pipia took office in 1721, became cardinal in 1724, and relinquished his post in 1725. The term of Bremond lasted seven years but those of Ripoll (1725-1747), Boxadors (1756-1777), and Quinones filled sixty-five. It was the unhappy lot of Quinones to witness the blows that fell after 1790.

In governing, these generals had little assistance from the general chapter. Apart from the meeting called by Cloche in 1705, it assembled during this century only to elect a new master. The Order was no longer accustomed to representative government on its highest level. Even if this had not been so, prevailing autocracy in the political order and the wars of the ruling houses stood in the way of holding chapters. Dominican representative government functioned only on the provincial level. Provincial chapters continued to meet every four years. After the general chapter of 1777, another meeting was not held until 1832, fifty-five years later.

The Holy See continued its close supervision of the Order. After creating Master General Pipia a cardinal, Benedict XIII, one of the Order's sons, designated the master of the sacred palace, Angelus William Molo, to preside over the chapter called to choose a successor in 1725. He also sent along a program of action. In 1756, Benedict XIV first insisted that the chapter be held in Bologna to honor St. Dominic but then decided to preside over the election and transferred it to Rome. Boxadors, the master elected on that occasion, found himself thwarted two years later when Clement XIII, who succeeded Benedict, obliged him to cancel a chapter he had summoned to meet at Barcelona in 1759. Pius VI was present when Quinones was elected in 1777. Before leaving the Casanate Library, where the chapter was meeting, he appointed Cardinal Boxadors to preside over its remaining sessions and granted him the right to vote.

The papal concern for the well-being of the Order did not stop short at the level of government but probed deeply into Dominican life. Benedict XIII's instructions to the 1725 chapter focused on many details that reveal a departure from ancient discipline, a development probably due as much to a growing difficulty in adhering to customs of an age long past as to a decline in religious spirit. He called for faithful attendance in choir, more fidelity to the midnight office, at least on the part of novices, and uniformity in clothing and diet. His emphasis on these points indicates the hardships that midnight matins, perpetual abstinence, and the long fast from September 14th to Easter were causing in a more affluent age than the medieval. More significant was Benedict's warning not to ape the fashions and diet of the day—an important admonition, considering the love of splendor and display that characterized Baroque life and art. Benedict put his finger on a more serious defect when he called for a greater readiness to do the works of the ministry and a greater willingness to hear the confessions of the faithful. He gives us reason to suspect that the friars were less than eager to tend to the ministry. Two years later the Pope's love for the

Order again surfaced when he confirmed its ancient privileges and granted new ones. His concessions were so extensive that his successor had to revoke some of them because they infringed on the rights of others.

The Provinces

The map of the provinces continued to become more complicated through the establishment of new provinces and congregations. The Order went into the century with forty-five provinces and left it with fifty-one. The additions came not by an increase of territory but by the division of existing areas. The weakness of the Hungarian province led to the joining of its priories to those of Austria in 1702 in a new Austro-Hungarian province—an entity that reflected the political union of the two countries under Habsburg rule. The Congregation of San Marco, which cherished a strong memory of Savonarola, achieved provincial status in 1705. The Dominicans of Sardinia, established as an independent congregation of 1615, became a province in 1706, as did the priories of Upper Germany in 1709. The distances and difficulties of travel in the New World induced the Order to carve the province of Argentina from that of Chile in 1724. The Observant congregations of Santa Maria della Sanità and San Marco dei Cavoti in the Kingdom of Naples were united as a province in 1725, a union soon dissolved because of disagreement among the friars. The Galician priories became a province in 1782 following the first partition of Poland, which brought that region under Austrian dominion. The Silesian priories, part of the Polish province, were erected into an autonomous congregation in 1754. Several other congregations were carved from existing provinces. The two pigmy congregations created in the French Antilles in 1706 and 1721 furnish an extreme example of the lengths to which the fission process could be carried.

The Nuns and Sisters

The nuns of the Order founded many new monasteries during

the seventeenth century, especially in Spain. For the first time in Dominican history, they entered Ireland, founding monasteries in Dublin, Waterford, and Drogheda. In New Spain they erected monasteries in Buenos Aires, Guadalajara, and Pueblo. Toward the end of the 1700's, the German province had fourteen monasteries and Upper Germany, thirty-five. In France, the Commission of Regulars forced the closing of some monasteries. Sensitive to current developments, the nuns, notably Sr. Cecilia Mayer and Sr. Maria Columba Weigl, undertook works of expiation to counteract the rationalistic denial of the supernatural order. Following an apparition of St. Dominic, accorded her in 1730, Sr. Maria Columba experienced the Passion every Friday, receiving the stigmata and wounding with a lance.

The sisters of the Third Order established additional convents. Two groups of sisters went as missionaries to the Island of Martinique. In 1684, Mother Maria Poussepin, aided by Fr. Mespolité of the Parisian general novitiate, founded the still flourishing Congregation of Sisters of Charity of the Presentation for the exercise of the corporal works of mercy. It now has a vice-province in the United States and four provinces in South America.

The Liturgy

The Dominican liturgy was enriched by the addition of the feast of the newly canonized Agnes of Montepulciano in 1729 and the feast of the Holy Rosary in 1757. The introduction of part singing and instrumental music into liturgical services may be an illustration of what Benedict XIII had in mind when he spoke against accepting the fashions of the age. Whether it was a distortion of values to look for musical ability in those applying for admission to a monastery, as was true at St. Catherine's in Augsburg and elsewhere, is for others to judge. St. Catherine's did not search in vain. On the feast of its patroness in 1719, two postulants blew the trumpet and the waldhorn for the first time during services. One of them was still blowing her horn thirty-five years later.

The Interference of the Secular State

The entrance of the secular government into the internal affairs of religious Orders was less benign than that of the popes. It became more virulent as the century grew older. The Orders were caught in the web that entangled the Church itself. Absolutism was now the fashion. The "enlightened" kings, captivated by the philosophy of Rationalism, became "benevolent despots" knowing what was best for their subjects without asking them. Rationalism's denial of the supernatural order and its scorn of the religious life underline the threat to Christianity that was implicit in the stance of these kings.

When the Bourbons ascended to the Spanish throne in 1701, the Gallicanism of France spread throughout Spain and its dominions, in Naples, Upper Italy, and the New World. Germany and Austria developed their own varieties of Gallicanism. German Febronianism was a radical attack on papal supremacy and advocated autonomous national churches under a diluted papal presidency. The Austrian program, set up under Joseph II, was called Josephinism. He established state sovereignty over the churches, claimed ecclesiastical jurisdiction, instituted arbitrary reforms, and suppressed many church establishments and religious houses. However, many of his social and administrative reforms and those of other "benevolent despots" were long overdue.

Trouble for the Order began in France during the 1760's, when Raymond Garalon, provincial of the Province of Occitania, challenged the right of the master general to undertake certain measures without the King's consent. Busy with his visitation in Spain, Boxadors entrusted the defense of the Order's right to Father La Berthonie, an outstanding theologian. Though the defense was successful, more serious problems arose for all the religious Orders. When twenty-eight Benedictines of the Congregation of St. Maur petitioned King Louis XV to do away with their habit and Rule, the general assembly of the clergy asked Louis in 1765 to petition the Holy See for the reform of the Religious Orders. Instead, the King created the Commission of

Regulars under the presidency of Lemonie Brienne, the liberal Archbishop of Toulouse. Three years later the Commission issued its directives for Religious. It raised the age of profession, suppressed religious houses with fewer than nine members, permitted only one house of any particular Order in any city, and commanded the Orders to write national Constitutions for themselves. The Dominicans were forced to comply in 1777. A national chapter of thirty-two prominent friars reluctantly assembled, under the presidency of two bishops appointed by the King, to fashion a Constitution. When the French ambassador in Rome presented their finished product to Boxadors, he flatly refused to acknowledge or approve it. He remained adamant even when the King pressed for approval, and the Provincial of Toulouse buttonholed the assistant of the master, begging him to urge Boxadors to relent.

The zeal with which the Commission of Regulars went to work diminished vocations and lowered the number of religious in France. Their measures accelerated a trend that had begun as early as 1710. From 1750 to 1790, membership in the Dominican Order declined by a third. In 1767 the prior of the Novitiate General reported to Boxadors that three of the French provinces combined had but three novices.

Joseph II, co-Regent with his mother, Marie Theresa, began to pursue Gallican policies in the hereditary dominions of the Habsburgs in 1765. He promulgated comprehensive regulations which forbade recourse to Rome without imperial permission, and publication of pastorals and other documents without the approval of the royal censor. He also suppressed contemplative Orders and monasteries and Third Orders. The number of monasteries in Austria, Hungary, and Bohemia dropped from 915 to 318. Joseph closed houses of studies and seminaries and substituted several general seminaries staffed by liberal professors. He seized church property, putting the assets into a general fund for the support of religion. His liturgical and devotional directives prohibited ancient devotions such as the Stations of the Cross and the Rosary, and even prescribed the number of candles to be burned during services. Not for nothing has Joseph been called the "Sacristan Emperor". The link thus broken with Rome was not completely reforged until 1852. The prince-bishops of Germany, especially the Archbishop of Cologne, Joseph's brother, Grand Duke Leopold of Tuscany, another brother, the Republic of Venice, and kings in Spain, Sardinia, and Naples aped the Emperor. Fortunate the Orders that escaped the fate of the Jesuits, suppressed in 1773 by Clement XIV under intolerable pressure from the "enlightened despots".

Philip Hughes closed his description of these events with this paragraph: "It is not hard to understand the French historian who writes: 'God now saved the Church by sending the French Revolution to destroy princely absolutism.' Certainly by 1790, outside the States of the Church and the new United States of America, there was not a single country in the world where the Catholic religion was free to live its own life fully, and not a single Catholic country where there seemed any prospect but of further enslavement and gradual emasculation."

Studies

The multiple doctrinal theories of the seventeenth and eighteenth centuries led the masters general to insist on fidelity to Thomism and to take strong measures to prevent the circulation of the books of two Dominicans, Joseph de Vita of Palermo and Sebastian Knippenberg of Cologne, who departed from it. Cloche, whose 1687 curriculum of studies had prescribed a complete covering of the *Summa theologiae* of Thomas during the theology course, continued to demand that every friar be thoroughly grounded in Thomistic doctrine. The 1706 general chapter discouraged the further introduction of the so-called "material" courses, based on manuals of theology rather than the Summa. The eighteenth-century chapters persisted in stressing the importance of Scriptural and linguistic studies and required professors of theology to introduce into their lectures material related to church history, canon law, and patristics. They were expected to ground their students in current controversies and drill them in the refutation of major heresies.

At his election in 1721, Pipia laid down detailed guidelines for safeguarding and spreading the doctrine of Thomas. A quarter of a century later, in 1757, Boxadors penned a vigorous encyclical on the study of Thomism and required that it be read at table every year as a perpetual reminder of the Order's mission to penetrate, preach, and develop a deeper understanding of the data of Revelation through the application of the principles and method of Thomas. Apparently the sympathy some French Dominicans were showing for Gallicanism and Jansenism spurred him to this action. Already toward the end of the previous century, Noel Alexander, the most prominent Dominican theologian in France, had encouraged these deviations by throwing the weight of his reputation on the side of both sets of errors. In 1684 Innocent XI had placed his *Ecclesiastical History*, a work highly regarded at the time for its critical acumen, on the *Index of Forbidden Books* because of its author's Gallicanism. Alexander submitted fully to the judgment of the Holy See and added clarifications of his text in the 1699 edition. After the editor of the 1734 edition added paragraphs and dissertations correcting the work's most offensive statements, Benedict XIV lifted the censure for reading it but did not remove it from the *Index*. During the controversy provoked by the celebrated "Case of Conscience," condemned by Clement XI in 1705, Alexander joined thirty-nine other doctors of the Sorbonne in holding that "respectful silence" was permissible in the face of doctrinal condemnation made by the Church. He also joined the Appelants who appealed to a general council against the *Unigenitus Dei Filius*.

In the bull, published in 1713, Clement XI had made a further attempt to put the Jansenist doctrines to rest by condemning the *Moral Reflections on the New Testament*, written by Pasquier Quesnel, an Oratorian. Many Dominicans were misled by the Thomistic terminology in which Quesnel clothed some of his errors and joined the Appelants. Others became outright Jansenists. In a determined attempt to cope with those who refused to accept the *Unigenitus*, Ripoll had to deal severely with the Dominicans of Rodez, especially Father Viou. Ripoll expelled him from the Order in 1744 for repeated acts of disobedience.

The Holy See encouraged the efforts of the masters general to uphold Thomism. During the first year of his pontificate

(1724), Benedict XIII issued his *Demissas preces,* a bull calling on the Order to keep alive and develop its Thomistic heritage. He commented on the leading theses of Thomism, especially those concerning grace and its relationship to free will. His letter to the chapter that convened the following year for the election of a new master emphasized the importance of unity in doctrine. Two years later, his apostolic Constitution, *Pretiosus,* granted the general houses of study the right to confer theological degrees on students who were not members of the Order as well as on Dominicans.

An important adjunct to Thomistic studies was Cardinal Jerome Casanate's magnificent bequest to the Order in 1700. In his will he bequeathed his rich personal collection of more than 25,000 volumes and made ample provision for its maintenance and the construction of a building at the Minerva to house it. He also endowed two chairs of Thomistic theology and a college of six theologians. The professors who occupied the chairs were to hold daily classes in the library, and the theologians were to assemble weekly to discuss current questions and solve problems submitted to them. They were to be drawn from the various provinces and their task was to defend the truth. The staff of the library consisted of two fathers and three co-operator brothers. The Casanate Library, which the Cardinal stipulated must be open to the public, ranks next to the Vatican among the libraries of Rome. It now has more than 205,000 books and 4,000 manuscripts. The Italian government took it over when it confiscated other ecclesiastical property after 1870. The last Dominican librarians left it in 1884.

Not only the Order's administration but also its scholars directed attention to prevailing controversies. In response to the philosophy of the Enlightenment, Salvatore Roselli published his multivolumed *Philosophical Summa.* Charles Louis Richard defended the religious life, the fact of Revelation, the sacredness of marriage, the authority of the Holy See, and the holding of ecclesiastical possessions against Voltaire, a bitter enemy of the Church. Richard also supervised the publication of the *Dictionnaire universel des sciences sacrées,* a work prepared by a staff of collaborators, to counteract the famed reference work of the *Encyclopedists*. The *Dictionnaire* was the forerunner of the later theological dictionaries. Before the troops of the French Revolution terminated his productive scholarly career with a bullet at Mons, Belgium, in 1694, Richard also published a series of volumes on the general councils of the Church. Other Dominicans who wrote against Rationalism were Valsecchi, Brunquell, and Jost. Thomas Mamachi wrote against Febronius, whose book did much to undermine papal authority in Germany.

Interest in the history of the Order developed during the seventeenth century through the encouragement of the general chapters and the publications of several writers. The most important fruit of this activity was the *Scriptores ordinis Praedicatorum*, published in 1719 and 1721. Begun by James Quétif and completed by James Échard, it is "an outstanding catalog of authors" and is still indispensable. "The most distinguished documentary collection of the eighteenth century" was the *Bullarium ordinis praedicatorum*. Thomas Ripoll gathered the bulls but was elected master before he could publish them. This was done by Thomas Bremond from 1729 to 1740. After his election to the generalship, Bremond assembled a team of historians to search out and publish other documents pertaining to Dominican history. Though this first historical institute of the Order ended at the French Revolution and published little beyond the *Annales* of Mamachi, it placed historians forever in its debt by collecting a great number of documents for the Order's archives. Another work of special merit is the multi-volumed but incomplete *Année Dominicaine*, written by Thomas Souèges, which records the lives of eminent and saintly Dominicans. Other scholars published documents of particular priories or provinces—Percin those of the Toulouse priory, Bernard de Jonge those of Belgium, and O'Heyne and Thomas de Burgo those of Ireland. A work of general character was the *Istoria ecclesiastica* of Joseph Augustine Orsi, a controversialist, theologian, and historian of high merit. He wrote it to counteract the Gallican tendencies of Claude Fleury's *Histoire ecclésiastique*. Philip Angelus Bucchetti continued Orsi's *History*, which numbered fifty volumes in the Roman edition of 1883.

In a century of great literary figures, Nicholas Coeffeteau ranked as one of the creators of French prose.

In the sacred sciences, Daniel Concina continued his twenty-five-year campaign against the laxity of the probabilists. His opposition often went to the opposite extreme of rigorism. Martin Wigant also wrote on moral theology. Thomistic commentators were Joseph Riedel, Willibald Mohrenwalter, and Renée Billuart. The nineteen-volumed commentary of the last author on the *Summa of St. Thomas* remained a useful aid to theological study in Dominican houses of studies into the twentieth century. Andrew Augustine Krazer dedicated himself to liturgical research and writing.

The Ministry

A number of outstanding preachers implemented the Order's preaching mission during the eighteenth century, notably Bl. Francis Posadas in Andalusia, Peter Ulloa in Spain, America, and the Canary Islands; Nicholas Riccardi, nicknamed Padre Mostro, Gregory Rocco, Daniel Concina in Italy, and Nicholas Coeffeteau in France. The German and Austrian Dominicans also boasted eminent preachers. The German Dominicans had established themselves in Berlin in 1681 to minister to Catholic workers who had taken employment in the munitions factory established by King Frederick William in Potsdam. They now extended this ministry to other mission stations in Prussia and acted as chaplains to Catholic soldiers serving in the Prussian foreign legion.

On the foreign missions Dominicans of the Roman province labored in Pera (Constantinople), Kurdistan, and Persia. The provinces of Latin America continued the local ministries that had been their domain since their foundation. The Holy Rosary province of the Philippines endured bitter persecution in Vietnam on several occasions during the eighteenth and nineteenth centuries and gave the Church large groups of martyrs. Its missioners were persecuted in China from 1745 to 1748 and during 1837 and 1838.

The Dominicans of Ireland, England, and Holland still worked under conditions resembling those of foreign-mission countries. Because the Protestant attempt to wipe out Catholicism in the British Isles had failed, and anti-Catholic bias had diminished, it was clear during the eighteenth century that the provinces of England and Ireland would survive. The Irish Dominicans had the better hope for the future. Though English Dominicans were functioning as a congregation without full provincial rights, the leadership of Thomas Howard had infused them with new life. His establishment of a house of studies in Louvain in 1697 held out the prospect of a return to full provincial status. The Dominicans of Holland, where the persecution had never taken the extreme forms it had in the British Isles, maintained its mission status and undertook to direct and conduct the seminary Bishop Cools, a Dominican, had founded—Roermund.

Conclusion

The segment of Dominican history that began about 1500 closed with the outbreak of the French Revolution in 1789. Except for the centralization that marked the Order's government from 1650, Dominican life continued during it substantially as it had for centuries. In the ministry, however, emphasis had shifted from preaching to the intellectual apostolate, which was colored by new problems and new controversies and a more active pursuit of the positive sciences. Provinces opened new mission fields and excellent work was still being done in the older ones. The liberal kings of the Enlightenment, who restricted vocations and closed religious houses, were weakening the Order constantly through their interference, and the intelligentsia were ridiculing the consecrated life and the vows, shaking the confidence of religious in their own vocation, and drying up the sources of new vocations.

Though the Order gave the appearance of strength, the absence of creativity within its ranks, except in some fields of scholarship, indicates a degree of stagnation in the departments of its life. Its theologians and philosophers were engrossed with the age-old controversies with the Scotists and those who upheld the Immaculate Conception, with the inefficacious Protestant polemic and the endless rehashing of the quarrel over grace and free will. These fruitless controversies absorbed the energy of able theologians who might very well have turned creatively to the problems posed by the Enlightenment. In the spirit of Thomas, they might have sifted out the positive elements and harnessed the intellectual, social, and political insights of the rationalistic philosophies for the salvation of men and the good of the Church.

The religious life, closely regulated by the Holy See, manifested no incentive, and, indeed, no awareness that it might be profitable, to explore whether there might not be new ways more in keeping with human dignity, of living the consecrated life. The men of the age could see no need of this, as the present age was unable to see it until the winds of Vatican II began to blow. The Order suffered from the malaise that gripped the whole Catholic body and was shackled, like the Church herself, by the liberal monarchs of the day. The eighteenth century was more concerned with the defense and preservation of old things than with the development of new ones. Soon, much of the old would be swept away violently.

CHAPTER X

THE ORDER FROM 1789 TO 1872

The outbreak of the French Revolution in 1789 opened a century of crisis for the Dominican Order. Quinones was still master general and the Order had fifty-two provinces, many congregations and monasteries, and about 20,000 members when the Revolution began. It was only the beginning of troubles. One country after another suppressed the religious Orders; in some places this was done by a single edict, elsewhere religious houses were closed step by step. Even though reconstruction began early, the damage was so severe and the disasters followed one another so closely, that it took a century to complete the restoration.

When the Revolution began in France, many Dominicans welcomed the change. They presented petitions to the National Constituent Assembly and permitted the Jacobin Club to hold its meetings in their library, a fact that gave the party its name. Welcome turned to disillusionment in 1790 when the Assembly suppressed religious Orders. Dominicans were imprisoned, exiled, sometimes killed, and hundreds of them fled from France. These events were duplicated when the French armies defeated the First Coalition of European powers. France took possession of the Low Countries and the left bank of the Rhine. German princes compensated for their lost possessions by confiscating Church property in Germany and closing many religious houses. By 1825 the German provinces existed no more. As First Consul, then Emperor, Napoleon closed many religious houses in Northern Italy and the Papal States.

Meanwhile schism was brewing inside the Order. When

Quinones left Rome for Spain in 1798, he appointed Pius Joseph Gaddi vicar general. Pope Pius VI confirmed this appointment and continued Gaddi in office when Quinones died soon afterward. At first, the Spanish Dominicans refused to accept Gaddi's authority, but obeyed when they learned of his papal appointment. However, some of them secretly worked against him. Needing no other justification, the Spanish government pressured Pius VII into making the Spanish-speaking provinces autonomous, something that had already been done for the Franciscans. In 1804, Pius divided the Order into two jurisdictions. Reduced to six years, the office of master general would alternate between the two, beginning with the non-Spanish section. A vicar general would rule the other part. Though the arrangement legally preserved the Order's unity, in reality each half went its own way. A vicar general began to rule over the fifteen provinces of the Spanish dominions, as yet untouched by war. Over the Order's Roman sector, Pius VII appointed Gaddi master general in 1806. He ruled provinces that were non-existent, or would soon become so, or were small and weak. When Napoleon carried Pius VII off to France, he forced Gaddi and the masters of other Orders to go there as well. With the fall of Napoleon in 1814, Gaddi returned to Rome, but his term expired soon afterwards. Immediately reappointed as vicar general by the Pope, he continued to govern until his death in 1819. Then, since the Spanish sector of the Order was entitled to hold office of master general by the terms of the 1804 settlement, four papally appointed vicars general governed the Roman sector until 1832.

In the Spanish sector, accordingly, Leo XII named Joachim Briz master general of the Order in 1825. The Spanish provinces were far from being in a healthy condition, having suffered very much since the beginning of the Napoleonic invasion in 1808. Many religious lost their lives and many of the priories were closed during the resistance to French rule. In Aragon alone 400 friars and nuns died between 1808 and 1815, and no recruits could be received. Known for their doctrinal severity and support of the monarchy, Dominicans incurred the suspicion and hatred of the liberal-minded elements of the population after Ferdinand VII returned to power. He weakly gave full rein to those who hated the religious Orders. In 1820 a royal decree suppressed all religious houses that had less than twenty-five members. Three years later the Government appointed a royal commission for the reform of the Orders, the prelude to their total suppression. Now ensued a reign of terror. Religious were set upon, beaten, often killed; their houses were invaded and ransacked. This happened to the priories of St. Thomas in Madrid, Barcelona, and Saragossa. Such was the state of affairs when Joachim Briz became master general. Owing to the independence movements in New Spain, he could exercise no authority over the Latin-American provinces, and they could not communicate with him.

The revolutionary governments were not kind to the Church. Those in Chile, Argentina, Peru, and Colombia confiscated property, forcing many religious houses to close. Unsettled conditions in Mexico, especially during the liberal regime of Benito Juarez, all but destroyed the religious Orders after 1861. Guatemala suppressed them during the liberal revolution of 1870. Nevertheless, Dominicans kept a foothold in all these countries.

When the term of Joachim Briz ended, an opportunity to reunite the Order was lost. Though the Spanish Dominicans wanted reunion and their King raised no objections, Gregory XVI decided that each sector should again choose its own superior. Consequently, in 1832, the Dominicans of Spain elected a vicar in general chapter, the first to convene since 1777. Conditions continued to deteriorate in Spain. A decree of 1835 freed religious from their rules and the Cortes suppressed all the Orders in 1837, an act that also destroyed the Dominican province of the West Indies. Only the province of the Holy Rosary of the Philippines continued to thrive. The liberal government of Portugal had already outlawed the Orders in 1834.

Voting by mail, the Roman sector of the Order elected Ferdinand Jabalot master general in 1832. He died two years later, but two papally appointed masters general, Benedict Olivieri and Thomas Cipolletti, filled out his six-year term. Conditions were settled to permit the election of Ancarani in chapter in 1838, and Vincent Ajello in 1844. Ancarani held an intermediate chapter in 1841.

The State of the Provinces

Restoration began in the provinces with the downfall of Napoleon. The Italian Dominicans had suffered heavily, Sardinia and Sicily had hardly been hurt. Sicily was healthy enough to permit Pius IX to carve the province of Malta from it in 1832 and to divide the remainder into three smaller provinces. Other provinces were not so fortunate. That of St. Peter Martyr was suppressed from 1802 to 1814. At that time, Lombardy annexed the surviving houses of the former province of St. Dominic and the Congregation of Bl. James Salomoni. About 1822, only twenty-five of the former 250 houses of the province of Naples were in existence. The Roman province had a continued existence but was very weak.

In Northern Europe, the Dominicans of Holland were able to assemble in chapter and elect a provincial in 1804. Granted permission by Pius IX to train novices in parish rectories, the province established a school of theology in 1824 and a house of studies in 1844. In Belgium eight survivors resumed religious life in 1835. After the emancipation acts of 1829, the province of Ireland had fifty members and was functioning normally, but the English province, though it now had full liberty to operate, was extremely weak.

In eastern Europe all the provinces but Austria were still in existence. In 1839 it was able to reopen the priory of Vienna. Dalmatia had been reduced to twenty-one members by 1821. Bohemia was in a better condition; in 1850 it numbered forty-two members and counted seven priories. The provinces of Poland, Russia, Galicia, and Lithuania fared well until 1830. Then, except for Galicia, which was in Austrian territory, they suffered greatly from the confiscations and harsh measures used by Russia to put down the Polish rebellions of 1830 and 1836. In 1839 the Order had to unite the remnants of the Lithuanian and Russian provinces. Its membership shrank steadily after 1844 and it finally became extinct. The priory of St. Petersburg (Leningrad) survived until 1914.

Three events now gave the Order hope of a better future. The first was the departure of four English Dominicans for the United

States in 1804 under the leadership of Edward Dominic Fenwick. At the request of Bishop John Carroll, they sacrificed their intention of settling in Maryland and went into the pioneer state of Kentucky. Gaddi organized them as the province of St. Joseph in 1805. Working under missionary conditions and experiencing great difficulty in gaining recruits, it numbered only eighty members seventy years later. In the twentieth century it began to realize its great potential.

The second hope was the reception of the habit by Henri Lacordaire, the noted preacher of Notre Dame. He enjoyed a European reputation as a fearless and independent thinker, a powerful preacher, and a prominent ecclesiastic. After completing his novitiate at Viterbo, he returned to France in 1840 and was soon joined by other Frenchmen, also newly professed in Italy. Determined to restore the Order to France, Lacordaire resumed his preaching at Notre Dame, attracting many vocations. He opened a novitiate and several priories before the 1840's ended and was appointed first provincial when France again became a province on September 15, 1850.

Vincent Jandel, 1850-1872

Pius IX offered the Order a third hope when he named Vincent Jandel, one of Lacordaire's first disciples, vicar general on October 1, 1850. Five years later Pius appointed him master general. The Order elected him for a second term of twelve years in 1862. He had completed ten of them at the time of his death. When he began to govern, the Order numbered about 4,562 members and had made some progress toward restoration and renewal. Jandel set it on a steep uphill climb that returned it to vigorous life. His energy, positive plans, persistent attention to the contemplative base of Dominican life, and determined implementation of the Constitutions were the qualities that made him a successful leader. For a long time, the Order had needed such a man; Dominicans had been waiting for someone to lead them in the task of rebuilding the Order. Seeing its actual state in 1846, John Henry Newman had asked, "Whether it is not a great idea extinct?" Lacordaire did not think so. Six years before Newman made his dismal judgment, he had looked more deeply and seen the Order's great potential: "If God granted us the power to set up a religious Order we are sure that after considerable reflection we should discover nothing newer or better adapted to our times and its needs than the rule of St. Dominic. There is nothing old about it save its history, and it would be pointless to rack our brains for the sole satisfaction of dating from yesterday." Having studied the Dominican ideal and history, he was convinced "that the sap could flow once more through the branches and that the French branch could renew in time the whole trunk."

When Jandel took the helm, the spiritual life of the Order had dried up and its ministry was almost nonexistent. Within two months, he outlined his program. Returning to Raymond of Capua's plan, he called on each province to found one priory where the Constitutions could be lived—regular attendance in choir, observance of the fasts and abstinence, woolen clothing, weekly chapter of faults, and full community life. To implement this plan he sent letters to the provinces and made two tours of visitation, going even into England and Ireland. He sent delegates to the United States, Argentina, and Chile. He organized the provinces, redefined boundary lines, and restored provincial rights when enough recovery had been made. In 1853, he joined into one the former provinces of Apulia, Naples, and Calabria; in 1854, the three in Sicily; in 1856, those of Austria, Hungary, and Bohemia, calling them the province of the Empire. He re-established the province of Belgium in 1860, of Holland, Chile, and Lyons in 1862, and Toulouse in 1865. He initiated conversations with the Spanish Dominicans and saw their restoration to full unity in 1872, five months before he died. With his encouragement, German Dominicans, trained in France, opened houses in Düsseldorf in 1860, and Berlin seven years later. The *Kulturkampf* closed these foundations in 1870. The general chapter of 1868 approved a new branch of the Dominican family, the Congregation of St. Dominic for the Education of Youth, founded by Lacordaire in 1852. A congregation of Third-Order priests, it was incorporated into the First Order in 1923 and merged into the provinces of France in 1967.

There were also setbacks under Jandel. As the unification of

Italy progressed, the Italian government closed the religious houses in 1854, 1866, and 1873. All but Lombardy and Rome lost their provincial rights. In the General Catalogue of 1876 only 114 of the Italian houses still functioned. This was a loss of 380 since the end of the seventeenth century. Thirty-seven had fewer than four inhabitants. As noted earlier, some of the Spanish-American provinces became extinct during the term of Jandel. Also, from 1844 to 1876, the Order declined in membership from 4,562 to 3,474, its lowest number since the thirteenth century.

Despite these losses, steady recovery continued under Jandel's firm leadership. Three chapters met under his presidency—in 1862, 1868, and 1871. The first set in motion machinery for the revision of the Constitutions, the second approved a preliminary text and framed five rules for the new edition; the third, empowered with a papal dispensation, modified the Constitutions to bring certain points into greater accord with modern conditions. Jandel published the definitive edition in 1872. Twenty years earlier, he had promulgated a new Code of Studies. Everywhere he encouraged the foundation of houses of studies, priories of regular observance, and novitiates. He authorized Lo Cicero's revised edition of Fontana's *Constitiones, declarationes, et ordinationes*, a necessary handbook for the day-by-day administration of the Order, and sponsored the compilation and publication of a ceremonial, processional, and antiphonary. In 1870, a heavenly intervention pointed to the necessity of the Order's ministry. For five days, before Italian troops of Rome, a wooden statue of St. Dominic at Soriano gesticulated and walked about as a preacher addressing a congregation, a miracle that inspired Jandel to send out a circular letter emphasizing the Dominican preaching mission. Before his death he consecrated the Order to the Sacred Heart. The feast of the Sacred Heart was added to the Dominican liturgical calendar and, in 1825, new hymns were provided for the feast of the Rosary.

Jandel's positive, well-knit program went far to revive the drooping spirits of many Dominicans. Three books contributed to the same effect. Illustrating the working of the Order's ideal, Lacordaire's *Memorial for the Restoration of the Order of*

Preachers in France crystallized the genius and recounted the great deeds of the Order, and his *Life of St. Dominic* captured the Founder's personality and spirit in an admirable manner. *L'année dominicaine,* a multivolumed collection of the lives of Dominican saints and blesseds edited by French Dominicans, recalled the glory of the past and reawakened family pride.

The Implementation of Jandel's Program

Jandel's program did not go unchallenged. From the time he became a Dominican, he and Lacordaire differed as to how the restoration should proceed. More in tune with the modern world, Lacordaire opted for adherence to the Constitutions, but held they needed to be adapted to contemporary conditions. Jandel wanted strict fidelity to the laws and Constitutions, notably the fasts, abstinence, and midnight matins, except as modified by the general chapter. Lacordaire asserted that preaching for the salvation of men was the end of the Order and that its ministry must not be impaired by undue emphasis on the life of the cloister. In all essential elements the Constitutions must be observed, but pending their revision, since in some points they were obsolete, the dispensing power might be used to mitigate the ancient severity for the sake of study and ministry. He held that Jandel's program was too inflexible, that strict following of the Constitutions would lead to decadence and not renewal. Also reading history, Jandel saw that lavish use of the dispensing power had led to abuse and decay. In France the dispute led to the introduction of the strict regime at Lyons and the establishment of the province of Lyons in 1862. On becoming vicar general, Jandel immediately implemented his program. He founded a novitiate of strict observance at Santa Sabina and brought members of the provinces to be trained there in the Dominican life. At once a storm of criticism and opposition broke out. The Italian members of the priory were not ready for this strictness. To settle the dispute, the question of observance was thoroughly thrashed out in the presence of both parties in 1852. In the end, opponents of Jandel accepted perpetual abstinence but not midnight matins. Finally, Pius IX decided the issue. Santa Sabina would recite matins at midnight; elsewhere the prior might fix the time. In the same year, the Congregation of Bishops and Religious had to declare that chanting midnight office was not a necessary condition for enjoying the right to clothe candidates in the habit. In the province of Naples, the fathers claimed that the introduction of the common life was a French innovation and smacked of Communism.

The general chapter of 1868 called on all priories to restore the common life; the chapter of 1871 laid down norms of observance for the whole Order, which were incorporated into the Constitutions. Many priories then began singing Mass, vespers, and compline each day; in Santa Sabina, Viterbo, Riete, the novitiate at Woodchester, England, and in the province of Lyons, the full observance was maintained. This was true to a lesser degree in the province of France and the new German priories.

Looking back after more than a century and the recommendations of Vatican II, Lacordaire's approach appears to have been the better. In advance of his age, he returned to the original inspiration of Dominic but sought to update its realization in view of nineteenth-century needs. Long before the Council, perpetual abstinence, midnight office, and the use of woolen clothing, and other ancient practices proved too difficult for most provinces. We cannot blame Jandel. In 1850, except for a few priories, only a semblance of religious discipline existed in the Order. Many priories had abandoned the common life completely and the private life was widely practiced. It was a herculean task to restore religious spirit. Though Jandel insisted on some non-essential elements, he viewed these as the hedges that safeguarded the fundamentals. If the religious life were not restored, the ministry would come to nothing. He and Lacordaire were in basic agreement. Both looked to the original inspiration and laudable customs of the Order. They disagreed on which customs were helpful and which were obsolete.

The Ministry

The revolutionary period and its aftermath were not a time of great achievement. Many priories and houses of studies had to close, no missionaries left for foreign lands, and scholars were dispersed. Nor could they complete their books or publish those that were finished. However, many Dominican ministries came back to life after reorganization began in 1814. Philip Puigserver, an Aragonese, issued a three-volumed work presenting the philosophy of Thomas in 1817. Louis Vidal dealt with social and political problems in his publications. From 1829 to 1839, Bishop Anthony Diaz of Minorca published twenty-nine volumes in defense of religion and the Church. Louis Brittain and Pius Brunquell also published in the apologetic field. Vincent di Poggio wrote in general history, Hyacinth de Ferrari in Dominican history, and Raymond Guarini in epigraphy and archaeology. After many years of research in the archives and libraries of Spain, J. Villanueva published his *Viaje literario,* a history of the rites and ceremonies of the Spanish Church in twenty-two volumes. Thomas Zigliara's philosophical manual contributed greatly to the nineteenth-century Thomistic revival. Dominican professors taught at the universities of Rome, Naples, Turin, Cagliari, and Macerta. In the United States, the province of St. Joseph, cherishing Fenwick's dream of establishing an educational institution, conducted three colleges for short periods of time: St. Thomas Aquinas in Springfield, Kentucky, from 1808 to 1828; St. Joseph's in Somerset, Ohio, from about 1849 to 1860, and St. Thomas Aquinas in Sinsinawa, Wisconsin, from 1859 to 1865. The province of Ireland opened a similar school at Newbridge during the same period.

During the first three-quarters of the century, two Dominicans served the Church as cardinals and many more in the episcopate. At great sacrifice to itself, the struggling province of St. Joseph gave five of its members to the episcopate. The Order contributed to the First Vatican Council through its bishops and theologians. In the pastoral field, the sermons of two powerful pulpit orators— Henry Lacordaire in France and Thomas Burke in Ireland and the United States—packed the churches. On a more humble level, Augustine Chardon revived the perpetual Rosary devotion at Lyons in 1858. Soon more than 100,000 members were pledged to the daily recitation of the Rosary. Pauline Jaricot gave impetus to its regular recitation by founding the Living Rosary Association in 1826, which Pius IX placed under Dominican direction in 1877. The proclamation of the doctrine of the Immaculate Conception and the apparition of Mary at Lourdes gave much encouragement to preachers of the Rosary and contributed greatly to its use by the faithful. The *Couronne de Marie*, founded by the Lyons province in 1860, was the first of dozens of periodicals devoted to the Rosary. A priest of the First Order and four of the Congregation of St. Dominic for the Education of Youth, among them Louis Captier, an eminent educator, gave Christian witness by shedding their blood during the disturbances of the Paris Commune in 1871.

The Missions

Dominican foreign mission work suffered not only from the troubles in Europe, which dried up the flow of new missionaries, but also from local events. Disagreement with local citizens forced the Italian Dominicans to withdraw from their station in Mossul in 1815, but they resumed work in 1841. Jandel entrusted the mission to the French province in 1859. Persecutions in Indochina (Vietnam) in 1825 and 1838 disrupted the missions there, but by 1845 the country was quiet enough for a new vicariate in central Tonkin to be carved from that of East Tonkin. During the persecutions that raged from 1854 to 1862 four Dominican bishops, a number of priests, tertiaries, and laity suffered martyrdom in Indochina. Several of these groups have been beatified and have given their name to the province of Vietnam. Despite the 1811 antichristian decrees of the Emperor, many Chinese became Catholic in Fukien. New persecutions disturbed the Church in China in 1837 and 1838. About the same time, the destruction of the Portuguese province doomed its missions in East Africa and on the islands of Timor and Solar.

There were also gains. The Congregation of the Orient, staffed by the province of Piedmont, was strengthened in 1829. It constructed a new church at Pera, Constantinople, in 1843. Raymond Griffin, an English Dominican, made a beginning in

South Africa when he arrived as apostolic vicar. During Jandel's tenure, Irish Dominicans entered Australia and Trinidad. The Dutch Fathers began work in the West Indies and South Africa.

The Nuns and Sisters

The revolutionary storm that broke over the Order forced most of the monasteries on the Continent to close. Some maintained a continuous existence, such as San Sisto e Domenico in Rome, Speyer, Regensburg (Ratisbon), and Nay. Some survived because they opened schools. Nay conducted one from 1807 to 1857. Speyer took up teaching, eventually adopted the Third Order Rule, and became one of the largest congregations in Germany. The nuns of Langres established a school at Potsdam in 1806 that attracted girls from Germany, Switzerland, and France. A contemporary of Lacordaire and Jandel, but who did not know them, Mother Dominic Clara Moes, foundress of the monastery of Limpertsberg in Luxemburg (1861-1883), offered her entire life of suffering and prayer for the restoration of the Order.

The foundation of many Congregations of Third Order sisters devoted to teaching and charitable works shed a ray of hope over the gloom and mediocrity of the post-revolutionary period. Congregations developed on the Continent, in England, Ireland, South Africa, and the United States, where the first began in Kentucky in 1822. There were fourteen in the United States when Jandel died. They were as widely spaced as New York, New Orleans, California, and Wisconsin. Three of these originated with four nuns who came from Regensburg in 1853 and opened schools. Thirteen of the twenty-nine now existing and one in Puerto Rico stem from these four pioneers.

Conclusion

The period of Dominican history that lasted from 1789 to 1872 was one of almost continuous crisis. The Revolution and the Napoleonic Wars reduced the Order to the point of helplessness. When recovery began in 1814, new blows again rained on the Order. However, it struggled upward and made important strides toward restoration. In 1850, Jandel brought leadership, a program, and hope. He remained in office long enough to be effective, building solidly and repairing the foundations. On these his successors continued to build, even when they modified his blueprint. The French provinces, especially, kept alive Jandel's love of observance and Lacordaire's progressive, intellectual spirit. During the twenty-two years of Jandel's regime, the Order recovered its unity, renewed its spirit, reorganized its provinces, reactivated its government, and extended its ministry. Its nuns, much reduced in number, continued their age-long apostolate of witnessing and prayer; its sisters, a new branch of the family, were unfolding a fine ministry in education and nursing. When Jandel died in 1872, the Order had faced the worst series of crises in its history and come dangerously close to extinction, but had survived and was looking hopefully into the future.

CHAPTER XI

THE LAST 100 YEARS
1872 TO 1974

Vincent Jandel renewed the Order and restored the confidence of its members. His revival shaped Dominicanism until Vatican II, for the masters who followed him built on the foundations he had laid. Though there were some setbacks after his death, the Order continued to gain strength; its membership climbed from 3,474 in 1876 to 10,150 in 1963. Then, during the next ten years it dropped to 8,115.

The unsettled conditions that followed the Franco-Prussian War, the downfall of Napoleon III, and the rise of the Italian monarchy prevented the convening of a general chapter to elect a successor to Jandel. Joseph Sanvito, provincial of the Roman province, became vicar general and held office until 1879. Voting by mail, the electors then chose Joseph Larroca for master general (1879-1891). He and three other Spaniards—Bonaventure Garcia de Paredes (1926-1929), Emmanuel Suarez (1946-1954), and Aniceto Fernandez (1962-1974)—and two Frenchmen—Hyacinth Cormier (1904-1916) and Martin Gillet (1929-1946)—spanned most of the century. But three masters drawn from other races introduced a welcome internationalism into the administration—Andrew Früwirth, an Austrian (1891-1904), Louis Theissling, a Hollander (1916-1925), and Michael Browne, an Irishman (1955-1962). These three were the first non-Latin Dominicans to hold the office since John of Wildeshausen died in 1252. Vincent de Couesnongle, a member of the province of Lyons, was elected in 1974.

The masters brought to their office a wide range of ability and experience; most of them were former provincials, including Paredes, whose resignation Pius XI demanded when he developed a puzzling inability to act. Theissling was the first master to visit the New World; he was followed by Gillet, whose encyclicals deal with cardinal points of the Order's life. Taking advantage of air travel, Suarez and Fernandez visited Dominicans all over the world. The administration of Suarez was highly personal. When he died in an automobile accident in 1954, he carried to the grave problems and plans known only to himself.

The masters developed their staff and channels of communication. Früwirth added a fifth assistant and founded the *Analecta,* the Order's official publication. The 1964 general chapter raised the number of assistants to eight, designating one for the United States, a second for Latin America, and a third for the provinces of Slavic countries. Besides the older officers of the curia (the procurator general, postulator of canonizations, and archivist), promoters were appointed for the missions, confraternities, sisters and nuns, and tertiaries. A syndic was put in charge of the Order's economic affairs. Cormier built a new generalate on Via San Vitale to replace the Minerva, which the Italian government had seized in 1873. Since 1936, the master and his curia have resided in Santa Sabina, purchased from the government by Paredes in 1929 together with the monastery of San Sisto e Domenico. Gillet located the Historical Institute, the Liturgical Institute, and the School for Novice Masters, agencies he created, at Santa Sabina. During the generalate of Fernandez, in 1969, the monthly bulletin, *Informazioni Domenicane Internazionali (International Dominican Information),* began publication. It has become an important factor in the spread of knowledge about current affairs in the Order and in welding closer bonds of unity within the Dominican family.

Though only one general chapter met under Larroca, that of 1885, they have met regularly since 1891 with two exceptions, during World War II and in 1952. The Holy See permitted the postponement of the 1952 chapter to allow more time for a proposed revision of the Constitutions. Other than European nations began to play host to the chapter in 1949, when it convened in

Washington, D. C. Since then they have been held at Bogota (1965), River Forest (1968), and Tallaght, Ireland (1971).

The Provinces

The creation of provinces in areas where there had never been one before added a further international note to the Order. These provinces enriched its life, broadened the representative base of the chapters, and broke the monopoly held by the Spanish, French, and Italian Dominicans since the sixteenth century. For the first time, provinces came into existence in Canada (1911), California (1912), Australia and New Zealand (1950), Brazil (1952), and South Vietnam (1967). Suarez prepared for the erection of the latter province by opening novitiates at Hanoi and Saigon. The Dominican presence in North Vietnam came to an end after the 1954 Geneva agreements. Elsewhere new alignments broadened the spectrum. The province of St. Albert in the United States and St. Albert in Bavaria and Austria began their lives in 1939. Separated from Austria, Hungary regained independence at the same time. The Order created the province of St. Thomas in the Flemish-speaking areas of Belgium in 1958, re-established Mexico in 1961, and Portugal in 1962. The Philippine Dominicans became independent of the Holy Rosary province in 1967. Older provinces regained their rights. Colombia in 1881, Germany in 1895, Peru, Argentina, and Betica in 1897, Bohemia in 1905, Sicily in 1906, Aragon in 1912, San Marco and Sardinia in 1934, and Naples in 1937. The general vicariate of Central Africa in Zaire (Congo), where the novitiate of Viadana was opened in 1953, the general vicáriate of St. Hippolitus in Mexico, constituted in 1971, and the general vicariate of South Africa in 1968, look to the eventual erection of provinces in those areas.

Though the provinces recorded a steady growth, once the difficulties of the last 100 years were superseded, some of them experienced a striking development. Holland greatly increased its membership and activities. Benefiting from Bede Jarett's vigorous leadership, England grew in numbers, made new foundations, and produced men who attained a position of respect and influence: Hugh Pope, Vincent McNabb, Gerald Vann. Record growth occurred in the United States. In 1880 there were but eighty Dominicans in St. Joseph's province and thirty in California. St. Joseph's had boosted its membership to 732 by 1938. After the province of St. Albert split from it in 1939, it still counted 545 men. It reached its peak enrollment in 1963 with 758 men, St. Albert's in 1967 with 569, and Holy Name in 1937 with 181. By 1974, St. Joseph's province had dropped to 543, St. Albert's to 425.

Some provinces suffered setbacks. The German Dominicans had just begun to rebuild, when Bismark's *Kulturkampf* of the 1870's closed their two houses. The French fathers and brothers were twice expelled by the Third French Republic, in 1880 and 1901. They survived by going into neighboring countries and founding houses there, especially in Belgium and Holland. They returned in the 1890's and again after World War I, when anticlericalism gradually subsided in France. The province of the Holy Rosary was temporarily crippled during the American occupation and the 1899 uprisings in the Philippine Islands. The Mexican and Spanish Dominicans suffered most severely. After the passage of the despotic Constitution of 1917, Mexico inaugurated a bitter persecution of the Church that eventually forbade the ministry of all priests and expelled all foreign clergymen. Spanish-Dominican houses had to be abandoned there. During the civil war that began in Spain in 1931, the Republican forces killed 245 Spanish Dominicans. The communist take-over in Hungary, Czechoslovakia, and Yugoslavia destroyed the provinces in the first two countries and restricted that in the third to work within priory walls. Though the province of Poland lost seven members and a tertiary in 1941, it has remained strong in numbers. James Devine of St. Joseph's province, Ludwig Paly of Germany, and Urban Martin of the Holy Rosary province lost their lives during the wars preceding the establishment of the Chinese Peoples Republic. The missions came to an end in China when the Republic destroyed the Church after 1946. Dominic Chang of St. Joseph's province died in prison in 1967. During the 1964 uprisings in Zaire (Congo), twenty-six fathers, brothers, and sisters lost their lives.

The Nuns and Sisters

The nuns and sisters participated in the general restoration that took place in the Order during the nineteenth and twentieth centuries. New Constitutions, promulgated in 1929, harmonized their laws with the Code of Canon Law. The most recent Constitutions, issued in 1971 by Fernandez, incorporated the principles and recommendations of Vatican II. They are especially noteworthy in being the first in whose drafting the nuns themselves played a major role. Attachment to the Dominican family and knowledge of one another is fostered among the nuns by printed bulletins published by five of the monasteries, three of them in the United States. An important extension of the Dominican contemplative ministry occurred when the nuns entered new foreign mission fields. Ten monasteries now dot the maps of Japan, Africa, Reunion Island, Pakistan, Greece, and Norway.

Before the French Revolution there were about 180 monasteries; in 1895, 150, including those of the Third Order Rule; in 1949, 213 with 5,633 nuns. The 1966 census lists 216 monasteries (91 of them in Spain), 5,550 nuns and 154 extern sisters, nine federations affiliating 132 monasteries, and 22 monasteries of the Third Order Rule with 1,043 sisters. The 20 monasteries in the United States of the Second and Third Order have an enrollment of 509 nuns (1974).

During the past 100 years, the Dominican sisters have become the most numerous branch of the Order, outnumbering the fathers and brothers almost eight to one. In 1895, there were about 20,000 sisters in fifty-five congregations. Fifty-four years later, there were 129 congregations, enrolling 40,444 sisters. In 1966 this number had risen to 46,310 and the congregations to 136. Two of the most recently founded are in Vietnam. In the United States there are 29 congregations and also provinces and foundations of Dominican sisters from other countries. In 1974 the total number of sisters was 14,385.

In addition to their educational ministry, Dominican sisters have founded orphanages, hospitals, and residences for the elderly, terminal cancer patients, and working women. They also provide home nursing care for the poor. In the twentieth century, the sisters entered actively into foreign mission work. Apart from their native lands, they are present in ninety-six countries; however, not all of these are in mission territory. In America, Mother Mary Joseph Rogers founded the Maryknoll Sisters of St. Dominic for foreign mission work exclusively, and many other American congregations have accepted mission territories. Since Vatican II, the sisters have diversified their ministries. Some have participated more directly in preaching the word of God, giving retreats either alone or with one of the fathers. Others are engaged as co-chaplains on college and university campuses.

To tighten the family bonds that unite the sisters and strengthen their ministry, the mothers general in the United States organized a leadership conference in the 1940's that meets annually. In 1972, the provincials and representatives of the fathers and brothers joined them. The mother general and novice mistresses of Germany have met occasionally since 1951.

A new form of consecrated life came to birth in Marseilles in 1937 when Fr. Perrin organized *Caritas Christi*, a secular institute. The statement of purpose of *Caritas Christi*—"to form and give to the Church contemplative and apostolic laywomen, in all walks of life..." clearly shows its Dominican orientation.

The Third Order gained new impetus during the anniversaries of the Order in 1916 and of St. Dominic in 1921. It received an updated Rule in 1923, and more recent ones in 1964 and 1968. International congresses and a revised organization, giving members more participation in decision-making, have strengthened the spirit of the tertiaries. The estimated strength of the Third Order in 1936 was 100,000 members, in 1966, 130,000. Noted tertiaries during the last hundred years were Benedict XV, Sigrid Undset, the authoress, Martin Grabmann, the noted medievalist, and Bishop James A. Walsh, founder of Maryknoll. The Society of the Divine Word, founded by Arnold Janssen in 1875, followed the Third Order Rule until 1884.

Intensification of Life and Ministry

The enlightened leadership of masters and chapters, helped

by instructions from the popes, intensified and deepened the Order's life and ministry. In 1891, Leo XIII commanded the Order to end the private life and restore the common life in all houses. Though the Order had often tried to achieve this end, and again met obstacles and delay, by 1907 it had virtually eliminated the private life. A strengthened community life, a deeper sense of brotherhood, and a more effective ministry resulted. Several attempts made by the chapters from 1885 onward to establish filiation of friars to the province, rather than to an individual house, met success in 1913 when Pius X put his authority behind provincial affiliation. This change gave the flexibility demanded by modern conditions in the deployment of personnel.

The publication of the Code of Canon Law in 1918 made a revision of the Constitutions necessary. Commissions prepared a draft text that was acted upon during the chapters of 1924 and 1926. Called to elect a master after the resignation of Paredes, the 1929 chapter took no action, a failure that interrupted the threefold procedure required for the passage of laws and threatened to delay the production of a final text indefinitely. To solve this problem, the Holy See decided that the text established at the 1932 chapter would have the force of law. The Constitutions so adopted marked a radical break with earlier versions. A fivefold division, conforming to the five books of the Code, supplanted the traditional twofold division. Obsolete laws were dropped, and those still operative were embodied in the constitutional text. Thus the three-century-old distinction between the "major text" of the Constitutions and the "minor text" of the ordinances of chapters was eliminated. Once again, the Order had a unified body of law.

The Constitutions of 1968, adopted in compliance with the instructions of Vatican II, represent a more deeply rooted renewal and updating, bringing the Order into conformity with the spirit and needs of the twentieth century. Returning to the Order's traditional collegiality and subsidiarity, and respecting the findings of modern psychology and the democratic spirit of the times, the new Constitutions laid greater responsibility on the shoulders of each member for the well-being and action of the Order. It is significant that this approach to the new era in the Church, inaugurated by the Council, was the work of a world-wide questionnaire, a congress of provincials, a commission representative of many provinces, and a general chapter that met in Chicago, one of the newest great cities of the oldest democratic Republic in the world. The Constitutions received final confirmation at the general chapter of 1974.

The Order has always considered the liturgical life a fundamental part of its contemplative vocation; its leadership has consistently been attentive to the performance of the sacred rites. During the past century, as new editions of the liturgical books were needed, the master general provided for their preparation, publishing several editions of the missal, breviary, and the other choir books. The liturgy was also enriched by prefaces of St. Dominic and St. Thomas. The feasts of many newly beatified Dominicans were added to the calendar, more during the nineteenth and twentieth centuries than throughout the rest of the Order's history. Though there were now too many feasts, some of them were most welcome, those of Albert the Great, Margaret of Hungary, and Martin de Porres. Also, the Holy Father proclaimed Albert and Catherine of Siena doctors of the Church.

The revisions of the Roman liturgy by Pius X and Pius XII necessitated changes in the Dominican liturgy. The adaptation of the rubrics of Pius X to the Dominican Rite, made by Bruno Hespers and approved by the Congregation of Rites, went into effect in 1923. Especially significant were the substitution of the Psalter of Pius X for the ancient monastic psalter and the removal of the obligation to recite the Office of the Blessed Virgin on weekdays. The duty to recite the Office of the Dead weekly became a constitutional, rather than a canonical, obligation, except for the four anniversaries. Since 1968, this Office obliges only when one of the brethren dies and in the house of his assignment. The restoration of the Easter Vigil and the revision of the Holy Week ceremonies were binding on the Order and had a stimulating effect on the brethren. The 1960 revision of the Roman liturgy was incorporated into the Dominican liturgy under Michael Browne. The liturgical changes introduced by Vatican II were so sweeping that pastoral reasons and the impossibility of publishing Dominican liturgical books in all the vernaculars made the acceptance of the Roman, and the abandonment of the Dominican liturgy imperative.

Other events deepened the Order's life. The renewal of its consecration to the Sacred Heart by Frühwirth, and its consecration to the Immaculate Heart of Mary by Suarez during the general chapter at Washington in 1949, strengthened devotion to Christ and his mother. Though World War I impeded the world-wide observance of the 700th anniversary of the Order's foundation in 1916, the house of studies in Washington celebrated it with scholarly and liturgical activities. Pope Benedict XV signified the event by publishing an encyclical emphasizing the Order's evangelical and doctrinal mission and praising its work. He issued a second letter in 1921 on the anniversary of Dominic's death, praising him and lauding his genius. Other significant centenaries were those of Thomas in 1874 and 1974, of Albert in 1880, Catherine of Siena in 1947, Antoninus in 1950, Hyacinth in 1957, and Dominic in 1971. The 700th anniversary of the death of Thomas in 1974 was celebrated throughout the world of scholarship. More than fifteen universities and colleges in America honored Thomas and his contributions to the advance of learning.

Missions

The impetus Jandel gave to the resumption of mission work gained strength as provinces recovered and reactivated their mission fields. In 1876, only nine provinces were sending personnel to mission countries, among them the province of the Holy Rosary that committed most of its 335 members to the Asiatic missions. As provinces became stronger they re-entered older fields or accepted new ones. In 1922, the Order was present in 20 mission countries, in 1947 in 33, in 1958 in 40. In 1930, 470 Dominicans worked in the missions. The number had increased to 1,175, including fifteen bishops, by 1966. Eighteen provinces manned fields in 1949; in 1965, twenty-four. St. Joseph's province sent out its first missionaries in 1923 after it accepted the territory of Fukien, China. When that mission closed in 1946, it entered Pakistan and Peru, and, for eight years, conducted the seminary in Nairobi. St. Albert's province took territories in Nigeria and Bolivia, the province of the Holy Name, a mission station in Mexico. We have mentioned the mission activity of the nuns and sisters in another place.

To direct its missionary effort, the Order promulgated mission statutes from time to time, the last in 1958, and since 1946, designated one of the assistants of the master promotor of the missions. Recent masters have encouraged the missionaries by going among them on visitations. The Order mounted exhibits at the Mission Exposition at the Vatican in 1924 and 1925, and in Barcelona in 1929. It held a Dominican Mission Congress at Madrid in September, 1973. The provinces have kept alive interest in the missions by publishing periodicals that carry accounts of the mission fields and describe the customs and traditions of the people among whom they work. The Holy Rosary province founded the first of these, the *Correo Sino-Annamita,* in 1863. The greatest setback experienced by the missions occurred after 1946, when the Peoples Republic of China closed all the missions.

The Intellectual Mission

The academic and intellectual life of the Order, which had been badly injured by the events of the nineteenth century, was again on a solid footing when Jandel died. The 1852 code of studies regulated the program in the houses of studies that were founded or reactivated as the renewal proceeded. Cormier published a revised code in 1907. The 1935 code, issued by Gillet, brought the curriculum into conformity with the requirements of the *Deus scientiarum Dominus,* an apostolic constitution of Pius XI regulating studies in seminaries and universities. Taking cognizance of new trends in the sacred sciences, Fernandez published a modernized code in 1965. The general chapter of 1974 gave it final approval, calling on the provinces to supplement it by planning their curriculum of studies in accordance with the needs of their countries.

There have been some notable gains in the academic field since 1872. After 400 years, the English Dominicans returned to Oxford, establishing a house of theology, and, ten years later, to Cambridge. The American provinces built and organized fully accredited houses of studies at Washington in 1905, River Forest, Illinois, in 1922, Oakland, California, in 1932, and Dubuque, Iowa, in 1956. During the past ten years these schools have entered into cooperation with nearby academic institutions, such as the Washington Consortium of Theology Schools. The Washington faculty became a pontifical faculty of theology in 1941, a privilege also accorded to the studium at Salamanca, Spain. The faculty of Philosophy at River Forest was recognized as a pontifical faculty in 1943. In 1919, the province of St. Joseph's founded and has continued to staff Providence College, Providence, R.I., one of the larger liberal arts colleges in America. A high percentage of its graduates have entered professional fields. Dominican sisters in the United States conduct seventeen colleges for women. The fathers and sisters have also entered the field of secondary education, administering and staffing many high schools. They have improved their professional competence by earning degrees, attending summer schools and spiritual institutes. Individuals hold teaching posts in institutions conducted by other agencies. Since 1959, the Dominican Educational Association has fostered the educational interests of the fathers and sisters.

Reorganized by Cormier in 1909, the College of St. Thomas in Rome moved to Via San Vitale and changed its name to Collègio Angelico. It entered its present buildings on the Esquiline in 1932. John XXIII raised it to university rank in 1963, naming it the University of St. Thomas in Rome. The new status was warranted by the development of its faculties. It added a faculty of philosophy in 1882, of canon law in 1896, and became a pontifical academy in 1906. Since 1950, it has founded institutes of spirituality and social sciences. The rectorship of Thomas Zigliara, Albert Lepidi, and Sadoc Szabó brought the school to a high degree of excellence. Its enrollment climbed steadily from 120 in 1909 to over 1,000 during the 1960's. The University of Santo Tomàs in Manila also witnessed the addition of faculties and a great increase in student body, which stood at 24,000 in 1956. After 1890, Dominicans manned the theology faculty and supplied some professors for the philosophy faculty of the University of Fribourg. The fathers of the province of France have staffed the Syro-Chaldean seminary of St. John at Mossul, Iraq, since 1877.

Father Marie Joseph Lagrange, one of the pioneers of modern Catholic Biblical studies, founded the Biblical School of St. Stephen's in Jerusalem in 1890. He gave great prestige to Catholic scholarship and almost single-handedly lifted Catholic Biblical studies out of mediocrity. The School publishes the *Revue biblique* and *Études bibliques*, has trained a continuous series of Scripture scholars, notably Louis Vincent, Felix Abel, and Roland de Vaux, and has made exceptional contributions to exegesis, ancient and Oriental history, and the archaeology of the Holy Land. Since 1920, the French School of Archaeology has been established there. In a related field, Vincent Scheil, who held the chair of Assyriology at the Institute of Higher Studies, Paris, from 1895 to 1933, gained eminence as an orientalist because of his work in Egypt and Iraq. He edited the sixteen volumes that deal with French excavations at Susa. The fourth volume contains the first publication of the Code of Hammurabi.

The French province also made an important contribution to ecumenical studies when it established the Istina Institute at Paris for Russian studies and the Oriental Institute for Arabic studies at Cairo. Henry St. Johns in England and Yves Congar in France, who also began the important *Unam Sanctam* monographs, were pioneers in the ecumenical field. In the 1940's, Felix Morlion of the Belgian province turned to another modern interest founding the University Pro Deo in Rome, which addresses itself to modern techniques and problems, especially in the field of communications.

Almost fifty Dominicans participated in the sessions of Vatican II as bishops and theologians. The contributions of Marie Dominic Chenu, Yves Congar, and Edward Schillebeeckx to the Council are well known.

The praise that the popes from Leo XIII to John XXIII have heaped on St. Thomas and his teaching filled Dominicans with spirit and enthusiasm. Seeing in the works and doctrine of Thomas a potent force for the renewal of Christian life, Leo issued his encyclical *Aeterni Patris*, reorganized the Roman Academy of St. Thomas, and established the Leonine Commission for the publication of a critical edition of the works of Thomas. Speaking of the "purest streams of wisdom flowing inexhaustibly from the precious fountainhead of the Angelic Doctor," the encyclical calls for the renewal of philosophical thought in the Church on the basis of Thomism, a system it perceives as an effective antidote to nineteenth-century Liberalism. In 1880, Leo declared Thomas patron of Catholic schools. Benedict XV praised the Order for giving to the Church the Angelic Doctor and for never having deviated to the slightest degree from his teaching. The Leonine Commission was soon entrusted to the Order. Its work is very difficult because of the thousands of Thomistic manuscripts, but it has published many volumes and expects to complete the edition in fifty years. Since the publication of a Spanish vernacular edition of the *Summa theologiae* in 1880, similar translations have been begun or completed in German, English, French, and Japanese. A new English translation, a collaborative work of English, Irish, and American Dominicans, is nearing completion.

The period from 1789 to 1891 were lean years for Dominican literary productions; the volume and quality of writing only began to improve when the Order's academic organization had been restored. Before 1891, the books published were mostly textbooks; after that date there was a marked increase in the number and quality of popular and scholarly books produced. The authors are too many to catalogue. Their writings are found in their books and in journals and periodicals. Much of the fruit of the Order's intellectual effort is found in the 320 scientific, cultural, and popular periodicals it publishes or edits.

The Ministry

Even during the most difficult periods since 1789, Dominicans remained faithful to the traditional forms of their ministry, especially preaching. Since the days of Lacordaire and Jandel, these apostolates have displayed new vigor and life. Dominicans did a great volume of preaching in their churches, on bands of missionaries and retreat masters, and during religious weeks and workshops. Preachers of note appeared in every province. To be singled out are the preachers in the cathedrals of Notre Dame, Cologne, and Munich, of the radio Catholic Hour in America, and individuals like Ignatius Smith, Bede Jarrett, and Vincent McNabb. A feature of preaching in the American provinces was the vigorous propagation of the Holy Name and Rosary devotions, begun by Charles Hyacinth McKenna, the apostle of the Holy Name and Rosary. Under the direction of Michael Ripple, national director of the Holy Name Society, a huge national congress of the Society was held in Washington in 1924. It raised the membership of the Society to more than a million and a half. The provinces of Aragon, Hungary, Malta and Australia have also propagated the Society. The Rosary encyclicals of Leo XIII and later popes and the apparitions at Fatima greatly stimulated Rosary preaching. The books Dominicans published on the Rosary between 1885 and 1925 tripled. Rosary crusades were preached in France and elsewhere during the 1930's and 1940's, particularly during World War II. Michael Browne founded the Rosary Center at Fatima in 1957, and the general chapter ordered the appointment of a promotor of the Rosary in every province. Rosary congresses were held at Fatima in 1954 and at Toulouse in 1959. The culmination of these preaching activities was a congress of Dominican preachers, held in Rome on the occasion of the centenary of St. Hyacinth in 1957. In 1972, John Burke founded the Word of God Institute, centered in Washington, D.C., to promote more effective and more biblical preaching. The Institute sponsored the first national congress on the word of God in September of that year.

    The Order also contributed prelates to the Church—cardinals, archbishops, and bishops. There were one cardinal and thirty-six bishops in 1973. Dominicans have served in the Roman congregations and as papal delegates and nuncios. Archbishop John T. McNicholas became one of the leaders of the American hierarchy during his tenure in the see of Cincinnati from 1925 to 1950. Bishop Louis Scheerer, who opened the Pakistan mission of St.

Joseph's province in 1956, died there in 1966. He also worked for many years in China.

Modern wars saw Dominicans serving as chaplains and soldiers in the ranks. Some of them were imprisoned or lost their lives, among them Peter Craig of St. Joseph's province, who was killed in action in Korea in 1951. The chaplaincy in Ohio State Penitentiary was held by Dominicans after 1893 and in the prisons of Washington after 1925. From late in the last century, they have been chaplains at the Soldiers Home of the United States in Washington. Francis Stratmann became an apostle of peace. Becoming convinced during World War I that war was simply not the Christian solution to world problems, he spoke out against militarism, war, and the atrocities of war. His lifetime dedication to the gospel of peace and his writings, especially *The Church and War* (1928) and *War and Christianity Today* (1956), made him a key figure in the German Catholic peace movement. He suffered for his convictions, going to jail and into exile under Hitler. He died in December, 1971.

The Order's ministry diversified after 1919. Dominicans entered the fields of theatre, film, radio, and television, notably Norbert Wendell, who conducted a television program in New York for many years. Stanislaus Gillet engaged in an apostolate among the actors of the French theatre. Urban Nagle and Thomas Carey founded Blackfriars Guild and Theatre in New York, and Gilbert Hartke inaugurated the highly successful Speech and Drama Department of Catholic University of America.

The general chapter of 1901 urged the brethren to be attentive to the material as well as the spiritual needs of their neighbor. Accordingly, Dominicans sponsored a number of social activities. Fathers Rutten and Perquy founded a school in 1923 to train workers professionally. Five years later, Ambrose Croft organized the first social week in Ireland. In Spain, where the fathers worked for the moral and economic betterment of working men, Fr. Gajo was executed during the 1936 Civil War for his Christian social activities. In recognition of his humanitarian work in founding villages for refugees, Henry Pire, a Belgian father, won the Nobel Peace Prize in 1958. Dominican interest in social problems is further evidenced by Joseph Lebret's movement and publication, *Économie et humanisme*, established at Evreux, Fridolin Utz's foundation of the Institute of Social Sciences at the University of Fribourg, and French Dominican interest in the Worker-Priest movement.

EPILOGUE

The century stretching from 1872 to 1974 witnessed the progressive recovery of the Order from the disasters of the nineteenth century and the extension of Dominican activity into new fields. Apparently close to extinction in 1850, it steadily gained strength, personnel, and confidence. The crisis that began with the French Revolution was the worst of the crises the Order had faced until then. It came successfully through it as it had through all the others. Having risen more than once from its own ashes to new life, it has reason to believe that Divine Providence intends that it continue to preach and teach the word of God, to believe that it has a ministry still needed more than ever in the era that opened with Vatican II. Progress in the fields of Scripture, theology, and communications and the fast changing tempo of the present time place a heavy burden on its shoulders. These changes make it imperative that its sons and daughters cling to the original inspiration that motivated Dominic, even while they modify their inheritance to align it with the present day and prepare themselves for the current strife. They must be both contemplative and active, consecrated to the evangelical life and dedicated to the sacred ministry.

The attempt to cope with the directives of Vatican II, to meet current demands, to rejuvenate its religious life and update its ministry has brought the Order into a new crisis, one that is different and perhaps more serious than any before. In a sense, the Order must recreate itself, while not losing its historical identity. It must remain the same, standing solidly on its foundation, strengthening its century-old walls, refurbishing its interior, adding new wings, and building new stories. Impatient men might say, "Tear it down, build anew." Wiser heads will recall what Lacordaire wrote when the world we are in now had just begun. He could find "nothing newer, nothing better adapted to our times and its needs than the Rule of St. Dominic. It has nothing ancient but its history, and it would be pointless to rack our brains for the sole satisfaction of dating from yesterday." There is a beauty about an old house and a spirit in it that a new one can never match. The memories and strength of a family live within its walls; its rooms speak of men and deeds. The men and women of old seem to walk and live there still, imparting their joy and strength to their younger brothers and sisters.

Much has been done since Vatican II, notably the enactment of new Constitutions in 1968 and the Statutes that the provinces have written for themselves. Much more remains to be done; the crisis will not go away soon. It will never go away. Human beings are so prone to inertia and changes come so fast that it will always be necessary to renew and update. A plateau, a static time, will never come again. The Order is a pilgrim like the Church and cannot afford to stand still.

Renewal has come and updating has taken place in times past only when fervent Dominicans understood their Order, its contemplative ministry, and the need the Church has for what it can do. They were men and women of prayer, of community, of broad cultural background and intellectual training. They had the courage to live despite crises that long endured. The record indicates that when the Order goes about its work resolutely, courageously taking up its ministry, Divine Providence blesses it, even during times of trial and disaster. Its history demonstrates the amazing durability of the evangelical life. The prayers St. Dominic poured out during his nightly vigils are still heard as he stands making intercession for his children before the throne of grace.

GENERAL WORKS ON THE DOMINICAN ORDER IN ENGLISH

For additional bibliography and reputable works in foreign languages, the reader may consult the books listed below.

ABBREVIATIONS
CE: *Catholic Encyclopedia.* New York, 1908.
NCE: *New Catholic Encyclopedia.* New York, 1966.

Antony, C.M., *In St. Dominic's Country.* London, 1912.
Barker, E., *The Dominican Order and Convocation.* Oxford, 1913.
Bennett, R.F., *The Early Dominicans. Studies in 13th Century History.* Cambridge, 1937.
Bonniwell, W.R., *A History of the Dominican Liturgy,* 1915-45, 2 ed., New York, 1945.
"Dominican Rite," NCE, IV, 982-93.
Clerissac, H., *The Spirit of St. Dominic.* London, 1939.
Dominic '70', *Spode House Review* (Hawkesyard Priory, England) (entire issue).
Dominican Saints. By the Novices. 2nd ed., Washington, D.C., 1921.
Dorcy, Sr. Mary Jean., *St. Dominic's Family; Lives and Legends.* Dubuque, 1964.
Frachet, Gerard., *Lives of the Brethren of the Order of Preachers,* 1206-1259. Trans. P. Conway with notes and introd. B. Jarrett. New York, 1924. Reprint: London, 1955.
Galbraith, G.R., *The Constitution of the Dominican Order 1216-1360.* Manchester, 1925.
Gardeil, A., *The Gifts of the Holy Ghost in Dominican Saints.* Milwaukee, 1937.
Guiraud, J., *St. Dominic,* London, 1901.
Hinnebusch, William, "Consecration and Ministry in the Dominican Order," *The Way,* Supplement 17 (Autumn, 1972), 58-68.

"Dominicans." NCE, IV, 974-82.
Dominican Spirituality, Principles and Practice. Washington, D.C., 1965.
"Dominican Spirituality." NCE, IV, 971-74.
Early English Friars Preachers. Rome, 1951.
History of the Dominican Order, Vols. I-II. New York, 1966, 1973.
"How the Dominican Order Faced its Crises," *Review for Religious,* XXII (1973), 1307-1321.
Renewal in the Spirit of St. Dominic. With chapters by James Thuline and Sister Marlene Halpin. Washington, D.C., 1968.
Jacquier, Père., *The Friar Preacher, Yesterday and Today.* New York, 1915.
Jarett, B., *The English Dominicans.* London, 1921. Abridged edition, London, 1937.
Life of St. Dominic. Westminster, Md., 1947.
Joret, F.D., *Dominican Life.* Westminster, Md. 1947.
Lacordaire, H.D., *Historical Sketch of the Order of St. Dominic. A Memorial to the French people.* English edition.
Lehner, C., (ed.) St. Dominic. *Biographical Documents.* Washington, D.C., 1964.
Mandonnet, P., *St. Dominic and His Work.* Ed. by M.H. Vicaire, Partial English trans. by Sr. Benedicta Larkin, St. Louis, Mo., "Preachers, Order of," *Catholic Encyclopedia,* XII, 354-70.
Mortier, F.A., *Histoire des maitres gènèraux de l'ordre des frères Prêcheurs.* 8 vols. (8th vol. is index.) Paris, 1903-20.
Mulhern, P., *The Early Dominican Lay Brother.* Washington, D.C., 1944.
O'Daniel, D.F., *First Disciple of St. Dominic.* Washington, D.C., 1928.
Parmisano, A.S., "Contemporary Dominican Life," *Review for Religious,* XXXI (1972), 211-25.
Pepler, Conrad, "English Dominicans—What Relevance?" *Tripod,* XII (1968), no. 5. The Eighth Centenary of St. Dominic, born 1170.
Pochin Mould, D.D.C., *The Irish Dominicans.* Dublin, 1957.

Reeves, J.D., *The Dominicans.* New York, 1930. Reprint. Dubuque, 1969. An excellent short treatment of Dominic's work and the Constitutions and character of the Order.

Regamey, P., "Principles of Dominican Spirituality." *Some Schools of Catholic Spirituality.* ed J. Gauthier, tr. K. Sullivan (New York, 1959), pp. 76-109.

Townsend, A., (ed. and tr.) *Dominican Spirituality.* Milwaukee, 1934.

Vicaire, M.H., *The History of St. Dominic.* Trans. K. Pond., New York, 1964.

Von Matt, L., *St. Dominic, A Pictorial Biography.* With biographical sketch by M.H. Vicaire. Chicago, 1957. Vicaire makes an excellent summation of Dominic's life and work.

Walgrave, V., *Dominican Self-Appraisal in the Light of the Council.* Chicago, Ill., 1968.

Walz, A., *Compendium historiae ordinis Praedicatorum.* 2 ed., Rome, 1948.

Die Dominikaner in Geschichte und Kirche. Essen, 1960.

Wendell, N., *Spiritual Powerhouse.* New York, 1964.